RACE, POWER, AND THE OBAMA LEGACY

This book critically examines Obama's presidency and legacy, especially in regard to race, inequality, education, and political power. Orelus depicts an "interest convergence factor" that led many White liberals and the corporate media to help Obama get elected in 2008 and 2012. He assesses Obama's political accomplishments, including parts of his domestic policy that support gay rights and equal pay for women. Special attention is given to Obama's educational policies, like *Race to the Top*, and the effects of such policies on both the learning and academic outcome of students, particularly linguistically and culturally diverse students. In a race and power framework, Orelus relates domestic policy to the effects of Obama's foreign policy on the lives of people in poorer countries, especially where innocent children and women have been killed by war and drone strikes authorized by Obama's administration. The author invites readers to question and transcend the historical symbolism of Obama's political victory in an effort to carefully examine and critique his actions as reflected through both his domestic and foreign policies.

Pierre Wilbert Orelus is Associate Professor of Curriculum and Instruction at New Mexico State University. He has received several awards, including the *Exceptional Achievements in Creative Scholarly Activity* (2013) award. Professor Orelus' most recent books include *On Language, Democracy, and Social Justice: Noam Chomsky's Critical Intervention* (with Noam Chomsky, 2014) and *Affirming Language Diversity in Schools and Society: Beyond Linguistic Apartheid* (2014).

RACE, POWER, AND THE OBAMA LEGACY

Pierre Wilbert Orelus

Routledge
Taylor & Francis Group

NEW YORK AND LONDON

First published 2016
by Routledge
711 Third Avenue, New York, NY 10017

and by Routledge
2 Park Square, Milton Park, Abingdon, Oxon, OX14 4RN

Routledge is an imprint of the Taylor & Francis Group, an informa business

© 2016 Taylor & Francis

Library of Congress Cataloging-in-Publication Data
Orelus, Pierre W., author.
  Race, power, and the Obama legacy / by Pierre Wilbert Orelus.
    pages cm
  Includes bibliographical references and index.
  1. Obama, Barack—Influence. 2. United States—Politics and government—2009– 3. United States—Foreign relations—2009–
4. United States—Race relations. I. Title.
  E907.O75 2015
  305.800973—dc23
  2015013081

ISBN: 978-1-61205-878-8 (hbk)
ISBN: 978-1-61205-879-5 (pbk)
ISBN: 978-1-315-67575-6 (ebk)

Typeset in Adobe Caslon
by Apex CoVantage, LLC

Printed and bound in the United States of America by Publishers Graphics, LLC on sustainably sourced paper.

Table of Contents

ACKNOWLEDGEMENTS

Chapters 3 and 5 partially draw on data from a previous study in Orelus, P.W. (Fall 2009). *The Agony of masculinity: Race, Gender, and Education in the "New" Age of Racism and Patriarchy*. New York: Peter Lang Publishers. Parts of Chapter 6, although substantively modified, previously appeared in Orelus, P.W. (Fall 2010). *The Occupier and the New Occupied: Haiti and Other Oppressed Nations Under Western Neocolonial, Neoliberal, and Imperialist Dominations*. Netherlands: SensePublisher.

FOREWORD

Mike Cole
University of East London

Pierre Orelus provides a compelling indictment of the Obama years with respect to both domestic and foreign policy. Orelus notes that while Obama, the safest and most pragmatic choice to follow George W. Bush, needs recognition for his progressive achievements on women's and LGBTQ rights, and to some extent (despite, as Paul Carr notes in his Afterword, its limitations and problems) on health care, he has followed and sometimes outstripped his predecessor in the pro-neoliberal capitalist orientation of his domestic policy and the pro-imperialist nature of his foreign policy. Moreover, having stated completely erroneously that there is *not* a Black and White America and Latina/o America and Asian America, Obama has not improved "race relations" domestically or internationally. Indeed, while his two election victories have symbolic importance for multiculturalism and antiracism, his stance on the deportation of millions of immigrants of color has worsened the situation in the United States, while he is accountable overseas for the wars of aggression against poor Black and Brown peoples, including the use of horrendous drone strikes. Obama's professed belief in hope and in change from the bottom up have been proved to be just slogans. Since Obama's record is dealt with at length throughout the book and in the Afterword, I will not make any further comments here. Instead, given Curry Malott's insistence in the Introduction that the crisis in capitalism is systemic, and accepting Orelus's

contention that racism in the United States is also systemic, I want in
this Foreword to address contrasting forms of power in another country in the Americas. I want also to compare institutional racism in the
United States with that country, a country where, unlike the United
States, the State is actively promoting antiracism and multiculturalism,
as part of an agenda for twenty-first century socialism. That country is
the Bolivarian Republic of Venezuela.[1]

In Venezuela, a conception of power, diametrically opposed to capitalist and imperialist power, has been formulated and has taken root. In
2010, stressing the prime importance of education, the late President
Hugo Chávez identified it as a key form of power in the ongoing Bolivarian Revolution:

> When we talk about power, what are we talking about . . . The
> first power that we all have is knowledge. So we've made efforts
> first in education, against illiteracy, for the development of think-
> ing, studying, analysis. In a way, that has never happened before.
> Today, Venezuela is a giant school, it's all a school. From children
> of one year old until old age, all of us are studying and learning.
> And then political power, the capacity to make decisions, the
> community councils, communes, the people's power, the popular
> assemblies. And then there is the economic power. Transferring
> economic power to the people, the wealth of the people distrib-
> uted throughout the nation (cited in Sheehan, 2010).

Of these three forms of power in contemporary Venezuela, the
first—knowledge—takes the forms of revolutionary knowledge and
the self-education of the people; of mass intellectuality and empowerment in the public sphere as well as liberatory processes in educational
institutions, both formal and alternative. A specific feature of education
in the Bolivarian context is the way in which it permeates the whole
society and is not confined to institutions.[2]

The second form of power—political power—can best be described as
a dialectical relationship between *el pueblo* (the people) and the president,
both Chávez and incumbent president Nicolás Maduro, whereby *el pueblo*
both inform the president and are informed by him through the revolutionary study and practice of both, and for which the synthesis is twenty-first
century socialism and anti-(US) imperialism (see Cicariello-Maher, 2013).

Like the power of knowledge and the consolidation of political power in the hands of the people, the transfer of economic power to the people in the Bolivarian Republic of Venezuela is about the transition from capitalism to socialism, in part via the creation of nexuses of power parallel to the state, entailing extensive economic power to the people, a revolutionary project that is profoundly educational and educative too. All these processes are, of course, counterhegemonic to the dominant global neoliberal and imperialist consensus. Socialist revolutions, as *ongoing* processes, are by their very nature educational in that for the revolution to move forward, there is a continuous need for a sustained intellectual critique of capitalism, an understanding of the dangers inherent in twentieth-century socialism and Stalinism, *and* the need to learn afresh as the revolution progresses.

With respect to the distribution of wealth, while mass dispersal of assets from rich to poor, from capital to labor has not occurred, the creation of a massive social democratic infrastructure, consisting in part of a large number of *misiones*—antipoverty and social welfare programs—under Chávez (first elected in 1998) and continuing under President Nicolás Maduro (see, for example, Dominguez, 2013; see also Cole, 2014a), has resulted in a reduction of the poverty rate from just over 50 percent in 1998 to just over 25 percent now, with extreme poverty down from just over 20 percent to just over 7 percent now. The national budget for 2014 allocates 62 percent of revenue towards social investment, compared to "social spending" in the pre-Chávez governments, which never exceeded 36 percent of the budget (The Embassy of the Bolivarian Republic of Venezuela in the UK and Ireland (2013)).

The Politics and Economics of the Bolivarian Revolution

In the 1990s, as a condition for their obtaining international loans—and even under threat (Victor, 2009)—a number of policies, based squarely on neoliberal capitalist principles and formulated in the United States, were foisted on governments in Latin American and the Caribbean. The "Washington Consensus,"[3] as it became known, was most thoroughly applied in Venezuela. In 1998, Maria Paez Victor (2009) describes how this affected the country: "This oil-rich country's economy was in ruins, schools and hospitals were almost derelict, and almost 80 per cent of the population was impoverished." In that year, Chávez won the presidential elections in Venezuela by a landslide.

Victor (2009) concisely summarizes Chávez's impact on the racist oligarchy on the one hand, and on the people on the other:

> Immediately the elites and middle classes opposed him as an upstart, an Indian who does not know his place, a Black who is a disgrace to the position. Hugo Chávez established a new Constitution that re-set the rules of a government that had been putty in the hands of the elites. Ratified in overwhelming numbers, the Constitution gave indigenous peoples, for the first time, the constitutional right to their language, religion, culture and lands. It established Human Rights, civil and social, like the right to food, a clean environment, education, jobs, and health care, binding the government to provide them. It declared the country a participatory democracy with direct input of people into political decision making through their communal councils and it asserted government control of oil revenues: Oil belongs to the people.

However, twenty-first century socialism in the making did not begin with Chávez. To exemplify this point, George Ciccariello-Maher (2013) makes a distinction between *el proceso* (the *ongoing* process) and *el presidente* (the president), the former of which he describes as "the deepening, radicalization, and autonomy of the revolutionary movements that constitute the 'base' of the Bolivarian Revolution," which involved individual and collective action by revolutionaries that pre-dated Chávez by several decades (p. 6). Ciccariello-Maher (2013, p. 274) emphasizes that almost everyone whom he interviewed in *We Created Chávez: A People's History of the Venezuelan Revolution,* as well as all those interviewed in the path breaking book *Venezuela Speaks!* (Martinez, Fox, & Farrell, 2010), spontaneously made this distinction. As one organizer told him, "Chávez didn't create the movements, *we created him*" (Ciccariello-Maher, 2013, p. 7).

Dario Azzellini (2013) describes the dual process at work in the revolution as follows:

> The particular character of what Hugo Chávez called the Bolivarian process lies in the understanding that social transformation can be constructed from two directions, "from above" and "from below."

> Bolivarianism . . . includes among its participants both traditional organizations and new autonomous groups; it encompasses both state-centric and anti-systemic currents. The process thus differs from traditional Leninist or social democratic approaches, both of which see the state as the central agent of change; it differs as well from movement-based approaches that conceive of no role whatsoever for the state in a process of revolutionary change.

Chávez's charisma and intellectual inspiration was a key element in the overall ethos guiding the Bolivarian educational project. It is important to stress at this stage, as noted earlier, that the Bolivarian Republic of Venezuela remains a capitalist society. In 2011, for example, the poorest fifth's share of personal income was less than 6 percent, while the share of the wealthiest fifth was almost 45 percent (Instituto Nacional de Estadística, 2011, p. 8). The full socialist economic transformation, envisaged by both Chávez and Maduro has yet to take place. Having said that, it is also crucial to point out that twenty-first century socialism *in the making* is apparent throughout the society, in the communal councils, communes and workplaces, and crucially in the minds and actions of the people in the barrios (large communities attached to major cities where the poor live) (Ciccariello-Maher, 2013; see also Cole, 2014a).

Communal Councils

We have to go beyond the local. We have to begin creating . . . a kind of confederation, local, regional and national, of communal councils. We have to head towards the creation of a communal state. And the old bourgeois state, which is still alive and kicking—this we have to progressively dismantle, at the same time as we build up the communal state, the socialist state, the Bolivarian state, a state that is capable of carrying through a revolution. (Hugo Chávez, cited in Socialist Outlook Editorial, 2007)

The communal councils, which discuss and decide on local spending and development plans, are key in the Bolivarian process. As Azzellini (2013) explains, communal councils began forming in different parts of Venezuela on their own in 2005 as an initiative "from below," as rank-and-file organizations promoted forms of local self-administration called "local government" or "communitarian governments." Following Chávez's landslide victory in the 2006 elections, and as the revolution intensified, "official" communal councils were created, consisting of small self-governing units throughout the country that "allow the organized people to directly manage public policy and projects oriented toward responding to the needs and aspirations of communities in the construction of a society of equity and social justice" (Article 2 of the 2006 Law on Communal Councils, cited in Ciccariello-Maher, 2013, p. 244).

In urban areas, communal councils encompass 150–400 families; in rural zones, a minimum of 20; and in indigenous zones, at least 10 families. The councils build up a nonrepresentative structure of direct participation that exists parallel to the elected representative bodies of constituted power. They are financed directly by national state institutions (Azzellini, 2013). Within a year, 18,320 councils had been established (Ciccariello-Maher, 2013, p. 244); in 2013, there were approximately 44,000 (Azzellini, 2013). Their objective is to submit the bureaucracy to the will of the people through direct participation at the local level. Committee members are elected by the community for two-year revocable terms and are unpaid. Ciccariello-Maher (2013, pp. 245–246) concludes—having noted that every council elects a five-person committee to oversee other levels of government at municipal, regional, and national level—that this is a powerful weapon against corrupt state and local bureaucracies that many hope they will eventually replace. According to the *National Plan for Economic and Social Development 2007–2013*, "Since sovereignty resides absolutely in the people, the people can itself direct the state, without needing to delegate its sovereignty as it does in indirect or representative democracy" (cited in Azzellini, 2013). The government also created the Federal Council of the Government (CFG), which is a link between the government and the councils, and where the two can decide budget allocation together. This empowerment of ordinary Venezuelans by direct participation constitutes a deep educational experience that is in total contrast to voting in a narrow choice of pro-capitalist politicians, in part based on their personality, every five years or so (traditional representative democracy). In participatory democracy people get to plan for the needs of the people as a whole. In traditional representative democracies, however, ideological processes of interpellation[4] attempt, largely successfully, to convince the populace that there is no alternative to neoliberal capitalism, a

deliberately mystified set of antidemocratic institutions, which benefit the rich at the expense of the poor. Schools and universities in the
capitalist heartlands are becoming more and more central organs in this
ideological onslaught. In communal councils, people are empowered. In
representative neoliberal democracies, they are disempowered.

Communes

At a higher level of self-government, socialist communes are being
created. These are formed by combining various communal councils
in a specific territory. The councils themselves decide the geography
of these communes. The communes are able to develop medium- and
long-term projects of greater impact than the communal councils,
while decisions continue to be made in the assemblies of the communal councils. As of 2013, there were more than 200 communes being
constructed. Communes can, in turn, form communal cities, again with
administration and planning from below if the entire territory is organized in communal councils and communes.

Workplace Democracy

The most successful attempt at the democratization of ownership and
control of the means of production is the Enterprises of Communal
Social Property (EPSC), which consists of local production units and
community services enterprises. The EPSCs are collective property of the
communities, who decide on the organizational structures, the workers
employed, and the eventual use of profits. Government enterprises and
institutions have promoted the communal enterprises since 2009, and
since 2013 several thousand EPSCs have been formed (Azzellini, 2013).

In June 2013, labor movement activists from all over Venezuela met
for the country's first "workers' congress" to discuss workplace democracy and the construction of socialism. The aim of the meeting was
to "promote, strengthen and consolidate the self-organization of the
working class, based on an analysis of its labor and an evaluation of its
struggles, to allow for the generation of its unity around a common plan
of struggle" (Robertson, 2013). As Ewan Robertson (2013) explains,
as part of resistance to factory closures and management lockouts by
bosses opposed to Chávez, dozens of workplaces came under whole

or part worker management in the last decade. However, the workers' control movement, which had the support of Chávez, has tended to stagnate because of opposition from management bureaucrats and reformist politicians within the Bolivarian process.

The congress, the result of a year of meetings between workers in different parts of the country, took up the slogan of the Venezuelan radical Left, "Neither capitalists nor bureaucrats, all power to the working class." The main themes of the congress were "the self organization of the working class"; "the class struggle and the state; legality and legitimacy"; "workers' councils, worker control and management for the transformation of the capitalist economy"; and the "formation and socialization of knowledge." The main goal of the congress was to draft a final declaration on the national political situation and on the labor movement, and to draw up a manifesto and plan of struggle. Again, the educational implications are obvious—the workers taking direct control of their own lives by composing a revolutionary program, analyzing Venezuelan politics from the viewpoint of labor rather than capital, making their own judgements instead of being on the receiving end of decisions made on high by and for the ruling class, as is the case in the UK and other neoliberal democracies.

"Race" and Racism in Venezuela

We've raised the flag of socialism, the flag of anti-imperialism, the flag of the black, the white and the Indian . . . I love Africa. I've said to the Venezuelans that until we recognise ourselves in Africa, we will not find our way . . . We have started a hard battle to bring equality to the African descendants, the whites and the indigenous people. In our constitution it shows that we're a multicultural, multiracial nation (Chávez, 2008, cited in Campbell, 2008, p. 58).

Arlene Eisen (2014a) has noted "the near total correlation between class and race in Venezuela." She adds:

> That is, nearly all the wealthy and bourgeois people are phenotypically European, while nearly all those in poverty who live in the countryside or shacks on the sides of hills in the city are Black and Brown. Demonization, animalization and

criminalization of people of African and Indigenous descent are themes both deeply embedded and flagrantly visible in the culture and institutions of Venezuelan society. White supremacy endures in Venezuela often resembling the United States and other settler colonial countries founded on conquest and slavery (Eisen, 2014a).[5]

Since the first presidency of Chávez in 1999, while significant obstacles and problems remain, major strides have been made to enhance the rights of Venezuela's indigenous and Afro-descendant communities (see Martinez et al., 2010, pp. 193–219).

Indigenous Peoples

In September, 2014, the Venezuelan chapter of the Indigenous Parliament of America completed final details of a report on the levels of inclusion of original peoples in Venezuela communities. Indigenous peoples were excluded for more than 500 years following the arrival of the colonizers. The report was presented at the World Summit on Indigenous Peoples at the United Nations, held on September 22 and 23 in New York City.

The document systematizes all the policies fostered by Chávez since 1999. Indigenous leader César Sanguinetti revealed the racist nature of the 1961 Constitution of Venezuela, which had only one chapter on indigenous peoples and gave the State gradual responsibility for incorporating indigenous peoples into "civilization" (cited in Telesur, 2014). Now, however, reflected in the Constitution of 1999, each original people "has its own cosmovision and its own culture." Sanguinetti also stated that "the revolutionary process has recognized the ancestral rights of the autochthonous communities and promoted their full inclusion." During the fifteen years of the Bolivarian Revolution, he concluded, actions taken to protect indigenous people "are not only included in the constitutional juridical framework, but have also been consolidated through the application of effective policies," an example of which is a Ministry with jurisdiction over the affairs of indigenous communities and peoples, one that is "unique in Latin America" (cited in Telesur, 2014).

Mision Guaicaipuro seeks to restore territorial titles and human rights to the numerous autochthonous settlements in the country. It exists to consolidate the Bolivarian Republic as multiethnic and multicultural. Its objectives are to:

- Demarcate and title the habitat and lands of indigenous peoples and communities.
- Promote the harmonious and sustainable development of indigenous peoples, within a vision that respects their different ways of conceiving that development.
- Promote the integral development of indigenous peoples to ensure the effective enjoyment of their social rights (health, education, housing, water, and sanitation), cultural, economic and political rights in the Constitution of the Bolivarian Republic of Venezuela.
- Promote, develop and implement policies to settle the historical debt to organized indigenous communities, and generate the greatest amount of happiness.

Mision Guaicaipuro provides comprehensive health care and implements organizational tools for project ideas, and for the demarcation of indigenous lands and the formation of community councils to promote socialism (Gobierno Bolivariano de Venezuela, n.d.).

With respect to language, as Lauren Carroll Harris (2007) points out:

> Article 9 stipulates that while Spanish is Venezuela's primary language, "indigenous languages are also for official use for indigenous peoples and must be respected throughout the Republic's territory for being part of the nation's and humanity's patrimonial culture." The 1999 constitution also affirms that "exploitation by the state of natural resources will be subject to prior consultation with the native communities," that "indigenous peoples have the right to an education system of an intercultural and bilingual nature," that indigenous people have the right to control ancestral knowledge over "native genetic resources" and biodiversity, and that three indigenous representatives are ensured seats in the country's National Assembly (these were elected by delegates of the National Council of Venezuelan Indians in July 1999).

Afro-Venezuelans

In 2005, Hugo Chávez declared 10 May as *Día de AfroVenezolanidad*, the anniversary of the insurrection of enslaved people led by Jose Leonardo Chirino in 1795. At a conference in Caracas to celebrate Afro-Venezuelaness Day in 2014, Nirva Camacho, a spokesperson for the National Afro-Venezuelan Front, reiterated a theme expounded by many of the speakers: the racism and violence of the Venezuelan Right, the Venezuelan allies of the United States whose aim, she argued, is to recolonize Venezuela. She then read from a manifesto that affirmed the Front's commitment to the struggle against colonialism, capitalism, and imperialism, and in full support of President Maduro's executive actions and the Bolivarian process (Eisen, 2014b). Maduro noted that "today's fascist ideas that attack society and attempt to impose a racist model of society are the same that have always denied the liberation of the peoples" (cited in Eisen, 2014b). He argued that the reasoning of the Venezuelan Right today is the same as those who opposed the liberation of enslaved people (Eisen, 2014b).

Camacho went on to call for a program of action:

> Considering that the AfroVenezuelan and AfroDescendant population in general still confronts the lashes of racism and racial discrimination, which are incompatible with socialism and the revolution, we propose that together the state and social organizations undertake to:

1. Incorporate racism as an element of analysis in the different forums dedicated to the construction of peace, since as an ideology it is present in part of Venezuelan society, especially in the ultra-right's close relation to fascism.
2. Revise communication policies in public and private media to eliminate racist bias, which would contribute to respect for our ethnic diversity.
3. Apply the organic Law against Racial Discrimination to persons and/or groups who incite hatred and violence through racist demonstrations, like those expressed in the terrorism that recently has plagued Venezuelan society.
4. Design and execute a plan to identify and articulate the variable of AfroDescendant, considered in the Organic Law on Education

as a necessary step towards the eradication of racial discrimination in the Venezuelan educational system in order to achieve equality for future generations.

5. Encourage a cross-section of ethnic perspectives as state policy, in all public and private institutions that give attention to the people.

6. Direct all levels of government and popular power from the Presidency of the Republic to those who administer government in the streets inside AfroVenezuelan communities, at regional, municipal and grassroots levels to evaluate and respond to specific needs (housing, health, education and roads) which historically are a product of structural racism.

7. Implement an ambitious plan of constructing Camps for Peace and Life in AfroVenezuelan communities, especially in the communities where narcotraffickers have manipulated our youth (cited in Eisen, 2014b).

In his closing speech, approving the principles of the manifesto, Maduro enthusiastically praised the various Venezuelan insurrections led by enslaved people as decisive turning points in Venezuela's anti-colonial, anti-imperialist struggles. He declared the whole nation a "*cumbe* of equality, peace and love" and went on to express admiration for cultures of resistance and happiness bred in the struggles of Afro-descendants in the Caribbean, Latin America, and North America. He concluded that the government would invest an extra 550 million bolivars to strengthen systems of popular culture, especially in Afro and Indigenous communities (Eisen, 2014b).

Undocumented Workers

As Tamara Pearson (2014) has argued, while "most first world and imperialist countries criminalize refugees and undocumented migrants, scapegoating them, promoting racism, and mistreating them, Venezuela welcomes migrants; and provides them with the same rights as Venezuelan citizens." While there are some problems because of bureaucracy and racism, the Chávez and Maduro governments, she goes on, have never blamed the millions of migrants on Venezuelan soil for any of the problems the country is faces. On the contrary, "migrants—documented or not—are welcomed and receive health care, education, and other benefits" (Pearson, 2014).

According to Article 13 of the Migration Law of 2003, enacted by the Chávez government, foreigners "have the same rights as nationals without any limitations" (Ley de Migración y Extranjería, 2003). Furthermore, in February of the following year, Chávez issued Presidential Decree 2,823, which instigated a national campaign to pay what he referred to as "Venezuela's historical debt to migrants" (cited in Pearson, 2014). Foreigners residing in Venezuela without documents could legalize their stay and become "indefinite residents." In direct contrast to the United States, police in Venezuela are obliged to help children without documents to get identification (cited in Pearson, 2014).

Ruben Dario, a general director at the UNES, a university for police officers that focuses on human rights, stated that Venezuela's migration policy "is distinguished for being tolerant, without any kind of discrimination, solidarious, with complete respect for all migrant human rights, and for not criminalising migration" (cited in Pearson, 2014).

Pearson (2014) points out that Venezuela has been taking concrete, though slow and small steps, towards a united Latin America based on cooperation between regions—one where borders either do not exist or are less prohibitive, and where no one is "illegal."

She concludes:

> Venezuela [is] setting an example for first world countries: showing that humane treatment of all migrants, documented or not, is easy and possible. Further, that the most important thing is to not force migration: to remove borders, to have cooperative trade policies (rather than the US's trade policies which impoverish people in Mexico, Haiti, and so on), and to not support the invasion and destruction of other countries, such as Iraq, thereby creating the refugees that countries like Australia and the US refuse to look after (Pearson, 2014).

As the United States prepares to lead a potential generational war in the Middle East (Symonds, 2014), as part of its strategy of a permanent "war on terror," an alternative to imperialism, neoliberalism, capitalism, and racism is imperative. Pierre Orelus powerfully demonstrates throughout this volume that Obama is not able to solve the crisis in capitalism and negate the racism that underpins it. As Malott concludes in the Introduction to this volume, the only way to save the world is to collectively negate capitalism itself. In the forging of both of these negations, there is much to be learnt from twenty-first century antiracist multicultural socialism in the making in the Bolivarian Republic of Venezuela.

Notes

1   Elsewhere I have written at length on developments in Venezuela. Here I will summarize the arguments in Cole (2014a).
2   See Cole (2014a, pp. 79–86) for an analysis; see also Cole (2014b) for an examination of alternative education in Venezuela.
3   The Washington Consensus was a set of ten policies formulated in 1989 by the US government and international capitalist institutions based in the US Capitol. It encompassed the following:

    • Fiscal discipline—strict criteria for limiting budget deficits
    • Public expenditure priorities—moving them away from subsidies and administration towards previously neglected fields with high economic returns
    • Tax reform—broadening the tax base and cutting marginal tax rates
    • Financial liberalization—interest rates should ideally be market-determined
    • Exchange rates—should be managed to induce rapid growth in nontraditional exports
    • Trade liberalization
    • Increasing foreign direct investment (FDI)—by reducing barriers
    • Privatization—state enterprises should be privatized
    • Deregulation—abolition of regulations that impede the entry of new firms or restrict competition (except in the areas of safety, environment and finance)
    • Secure intellectual property rights (IPR)—without excessive costs and available to the informal sector
    • Reduced role for the state (World Health Organization, 2014).

4   Interpellation is the *process* by which the legitimation, values, and attitudes required by capitalism are instilled in the populace. Interpellation is the concept Althusser (1971, p. 174) used to describe the way in which ruling-class ideology is upheld and the class consciousness of the working class—that class' awareness of its structural location in capitalist society—undermined. Interpellation makes us think that ruling class capitalist values are actually congruent with our values as *individuals*.
5   Animalization was racist with respect to Chávez, who was proud of his African roots ("Miko Mandante"—"Ape Commander" a mocking of the affectionate address of the working-class "Mi Commandante") and classist as far as incumbent President Nicolás Maduro, proud of his working-class roots, is concerned ("Maduro/burro"—"Maduro/donkey") (Eisen, 2014a).

References

Althusser, L. (1971). Ideology and ideological state apparatuses. In *Lenin and philosophy and other essays* (B. Brewster, Trans.). London: New Left Books. Retrieved from http://www.marx2mao.com/Other/LPOE70NB.html

Azzellini, D. (2013, June 30). The communal state: Communal councils, communes, and workplace democracy. *Venezuelanalysis.com*. Retrieved from http://venezuelanalysis.com/analysis/9787

Campbell, N. (2008). 'When the Supermodel Met the Potentate Naomi Campbell Interviews Hugo Chávez', GQ Magazine, February.

Ciccariello-Maher, G. (2013). *We created Chávez: A people's history of the Venezuelan revolution*. Durham, NC: Duke University Press.

Cole, M. (2014a). The Bolivarian Republic of Venezuela: Education and twenty-first century socialism. In S. C. Motta & M. Cole (Eds.), *Constructing twenty-first-century socialism in Latin America: The role of radical education*. New York: Palgrave Macmillan.

Cole, M. (2014b). The alternative school of community organization and communicational development, Barrio Pueblo Nuevo, Mérida, Venezuela. In S. C. Motta & M. Cole (Eds.), *Constructing twenty-first-century socialism in Latin America: The role of radical education*. New York: Palgrave Macmillan.

Dominguez, F. (2013). Education for the creation of a New Venezuela. In S. C. Motta & M. Cole (Eds.), *Education and social change in Latin America* (pp. 123–137). New York: Palgrave Macmillan.

Eisen, A. (2014a, March 27). Racism sin vergüenza in the Venezuelan counter-revolution. *Venezuelanalysis.com*. Retrieved from http://venezuelanalysis.com/analysis/10547

Eisen, A. (2014b, May 12). Venezuela's afro descendent front proposes program of action to confront racism and fascism. *Venezuelanalysis.com*. Retrieved from http://venezuelanalysis.com/analysis/10680

The Embassy of the Bolivarian Republic of Venezuela in the UK and Ireland. (2013). Retrieved from http://embavenez.co.uk/?q=content/62-venezuelas-2014-budget-allocated-social-investment

Gobierno Bolivariano de Venezuela. (n.d.). Mision Guaicaipuro. Retrieved from http://ceims.mppre.gob.ve/index.php?option=com_content&view=article&id=54:m

Harris, L. C. (2007). Real rights and recognition replace racism in Venezuela Green Left https://www.greenleft.org.au/node/37929

Instituto Nacional de Estadística. (2011). Retrieved from http://www.ine.gov.ve/documentos/Boletines_Electronicos/Estadisticas_Sociales_y_Amb

Ley de Migración y Extranjería. (2003). PROVEA. Retrieved from http://www.derechos.org.ve/pw/wp-content/uploads/ley_migraci%C3%B3n.pdf

Martinez, C., Fox, M., & Farrell, J. (2010). *Venezuela speaks! Voices from the grassroots*. Oakland, CA: PM Press.

Pearson, T. (2014, April 10). Undocumented migrants in Venezuela have more rights than US citizens in the US. *Venezuelanalysis.com*. Retrieved from http://venezuelanalysis.com/analysis/10599

Robertson, E. (2013). Venezuela: Workers' control congress: "Neither capitalists nor bureaucrats, all power to the working class." Links: International Journal of Socialist Renewal. Retrieved from http://links.org.au/node/3415

Sheehan, C. (2010, March 30). Transcript of Cindy Sheehan's interview with Hugo Chavez. *Venezuelanalyis.com*. Retrieved from http://venezuelanalysis.com/analysis/5233

Socialist Outlook Editorial. (2007). Chavez: "I also am a Trotskyist." *Socialist Outlook, 11*(Spring). Retrieved from http://www.isg-fi.org.uk/spip.php?article430

Symonds, P. (2014, September 17). US prepares for "generational" war in the Middle East. *World Socialist*. Retrieved from http://www.wsws.org/en/articles/2014/09/17/iraq-s17.html

Telesur. (2014, September 17). Venezuela to present report on indigenous rights at UN. *Venezuelanalysis.com*. Retrieved from http://venezuelanalysis.com/news/10916

Victor, M.P. (2009, December 4). *From conquistadores, dictators and multinationals to the Bolivarian revolution*. Keynote speech at the Conference on Land and Freedom, of the Caribbean Studies Program, University of Toronto, October 31. *Venezuelanalyis.com*. Retrieved from http://www.venezuelanalysis.com/analysis/4979

World Health Organization. (2014). Washington consensus. Retrieved from http://www.who.int/trade/glossary/story094/en/

INTRODUCTION
The State in Capital's Period of Permanent Decline
Contextualizing Obama

Curry Malott
West Chester University of Pennsylvania

István Mészáros (2011), writing and speaking since the 1960s, argues that in the current crisis, as capital's structural determinations push it ever closer to apocalyptic destruction, the State is called upon to serve a kind of *hybrid* role regulating production and intervening on behalf of capital's long-term interests. However, Mészáros (2011) is clear that such counteracting tactics might slow down capital's self-destruction, but it cannot resolve or reverse it. Mészáros (2011) argues that unlike previous crises marked by distinct periods of growth and recovery, such as the Great Depression followed by the post–World War II boom era, the current crisis is not *cyclical*, but *systemic*, and thus far more serious and permanent, ultimately threatening the survivability of humanity and the natural ecosystems more generally. Consequently, to slow down growing rebellions and the violent destruction of the capitalist system, even though evidence seems to point to the conclusion that no efforts can reverse capital's current "irreversible descending phase" (Mészáros, 2011, p. 19), the elite architects of capital have, nevertheless, desperately increased State intervention (i.e. neo-Keynesian and Neoliberal) in the form of corporate bailouts, tax breaks, militarization, and incarceration, as well as escalated social control mechanisms through relentless propaganda campaigns and advertisements in the media, military, and in education.

Other Marxists, such as David Harvey (2014), point to the ways capital is always relocating through a process of investment (often accompanied by some form of military intervention), disinvestment, and later on reinvestment as capital expands and contracts driven by the rise and fall of the rate of accumulation (i.e. the expansion of surplus value). From this perspective, capitalism could exist into theoretical perpetuity as long as the natural ecosystems can continue to withstand the relentless productive consumption of the self-expansion of capital. Harvey's work here offers a more concrete understanding for working class intervention for he does not paint a picture of a closed system, unavoidably determined by its own internal trajectory.

While Harvey's work here offers important insights, it lacks the more revolutionary global framework offered by the US-based Party for Socialism and Liberation (PSL) (2015). The PSL offers perhaps the most compelling statement on the current stage of capitalist development and trajectory, situated in an historical context.

The competitive drive among capitalists for progressively greater and cheaper sources of labor power, raw materials, and new markets led to a series of stages or eras identified by V.I. Lenin in his globally influential pamphlet, *Imperialism: The Highest Stage of Capitalism*, and recently updated in a book by the Party for Socialism and Liberation (PSL) (2015), *Imperialism in the Twenty First Century: Updating Lenin's Theory a Century Later*. Summarizing this movement of capital Lenin argued that during Marx's time capitalists competed amongst themselves nationally in leading capitalist nations, the United States, England, France, and Germany in particular, which led to national monopolies. The General Law of Accumulation identified by Marx (1867/1967) then led capitalist nations to face each other in competition over the dividing up of Africa and East Asia in particular. The imperialist nations, argued Lenin, underwent significant shifts such as exporting capital rather than products of labor, which was made possible by the merging of bank capital with industrial capital giving way to financial capital, which occurred during capital's earlier monopoly phase of development. Imperialist capital was becoming a more globalized and dominating force (PSL, 2015).

Lenin emphasized how such imperialist tendencies emerged within competing capitalist nations not as the product of particular policy choices, but as a result of the internal laws of capitalist accumulation that Marx (1867/1967) repeatedly pointed out acted upon individual capitalists as an external coercive force (PSL, 2015). In fact, in every stage of the development of capital the laws of accumulation compel capitalists to act in particular kinds of savage ways or be driven out of business by their competitors. This tendency remains true today. In other words, US imperialism is not the product of a group of evil Republicans and corrupted Democrats who have subverted the "democratic" process, but rather reflect the current stage in the historical development of capital, which can only be temporarily slowed down; it cannot be reformed out of capital. Only a worldwide working-class revolution can transcend the General Law of Accumulation that is the primary driving force behind imperialist capitalism.

Once the world was divided up into colonies controlled by the Imperialist nations, the only path to the ongoing expansion required by capital's laws of accumulation, beyond revolutions in production, was for nations to encroach on each other's colonial territories, which Lenin correctly predicted would lead to the world wars. After World War II the Soviet Union emerged stronger than ever, giving way to a global working-class socialist camp with Soviet supported socialist countries all over the world. The so-called Cold War consisted of the United States and its supporting countries waging a global class war on the socialist bloc. Once the Soviet Union fell, the United States emerged as the world's single capitalist super power targeting independent peripheral capitalist nations able to survive under the protection of the socialist bloc. Today's communist global movement must target US imperialism, which continues to be driven by the General Law of Accumulation (Marx, 1867/1967).

It is within this context, in 2008, that the capitalist class saw within Obama a temporary solution to the growing frustration amid sky-rocketing poverty and immiseration directed at the administration of George W. Bush while simultaneously continuing the global class war against independent and socialist states. Like Roosevelt and the New Deal of the Great Depression, Obama temporarily restored a degree of working-class confidence in the American system. However, unlike in previous eras, today there has been no economic recovery, only growing immiseration and wars of conquest. The imagery and message of the Obama administration as the deliverer of hope and change has consequently faded and its cynical and deceptive original intention has revealed itself as surely as the highly exaggerated staged bouts between professional wrestlers. As with education and immigration policy, the Obama administration as equally revealed itself as no friend of the working classes. It should therefore be no surprise that the most widespread era of uprisings and rebellions, sparked by state-sanctioned police murders of Black Americans, has emerged at the end of Obama's eight-year run. As working-class people, especially those who have been the most scapegoated, miseducated, impoverished, imprisoned and killed, develop a militant consciousness and revolutionary practice, the hope for a postcapitalist future accelerates proportionately.

Pierre Orelus' important book, *Race, Power, and the Obama Legacy*, offers a detailed challenge to the many false assumptions surrounding Obama. Complicating the situation, as Orelus highlights, is the personal racism directed at President Obama, which provides the appearance that it is just a few bad apples irrationally lashing out at the new postracial society that now exists. Not only does Orelus provide the necessary evidence to counter the notion that institutional racism has been eradicated, but he connects racism to capitalism. That is, race has successfully divided all those toiling millions who rely on wages to survive. Challenging capitalism therefore requires a commitment to dealing with the racial tensions that continue to fester within the social universe of capital, and within the United States in particular. Confronting America's racist legacy, however important that is, is also not enough. Critical pedagogues must also develop a deep understanding of capitalism, and the global class war itself.

Engels' (1880/2007) work against utopian socialists in his book, *Socialism: Utopian and Scientific*, offers an important analysis here. For example, Engels (1880/2007) argues that the utopian's response to the immiseration engendered by early capitalism demonstrated their lack of understanding of the internal logic of capital. Consider:

> The socialism of earlier days certainly criticized the existing capitalistic mode of production and its consequences. But it

could not explain them and therefore could not get mastery of them. It could only simply reject them as bad. The more strongly this earlier socialism denounced the exploitation of the working class, inevitable under capitalism, the less able was it clearly to show in what this exploitation consisted and how it arose (p. 70).

Critical pedagogy, in the present era, without Marx, suffers from this shortsightedness. Because mainstream critical pedagogy is based on a rejection of Marx, critical pedagogy tends to be based on simplistic understandings of social class that stress the consequences of capitalism, such as poverty, inequality, and in education, educational inequality, without grasping the dialectical nature of capitalism. Rather than explaining the barrier to becoming the capitalistic process of creating wealth through the permanent and extending separation between mental labor and manual labor, that is, the alienation of the labor-capital relationship and the extreme division of labor, critical pedagogy focuses on attaining social justice, equity, and equality within capitalism. A deeper understanding of capitalism therefore helps uncover the absurdity within the assumption that the Obama presidency could represent bourgeois society making good on its promises of equality and freedom.

Making this point even more solid, Engels (1880/2007) argues that human energies directed at contributing to a postcapitalist future should not be limited to abstract reasoning, but should focus on collecting evidence and analyzing concrete, material conditions, what he calls "the stubborn facts of the existing system of production" (p. 72). As with Marx, Engel's (1880/2007) conception of change is dialectical, marked by a dynamic interaction and antagonism between the parts and the whole. For example, social classes are antagonistically related parts of a larger whole mediated by the structural determinations of the mode of production. Engel's (1880/2007) shows this complex relationship in his description of the transition from feudalism to capitalism. In his discussion he identifies the bourgeoisie as the active, human agent of change:

The bourgeoisie broke up the feudal system and built upon its ruins the capitalist order of society, the kingdom of free competition, of personal liberty, of the equality before the law of all commodity owners, of all the rest of the capitalist blessings (Engels, 1880/2007, p. 72).

As with the transition from feudalism to capitalism, there too will be active revolutionary agents of change with the transition out of capitalism. What is uncertain, however, is the nature of this movement. That is, will it be progressive or reactionary? Due to the long-term negative effects of cultural hegemony on labor, a postcapitalist future could very well be more authoritarian and fascist than the authoritarianism and fascism of today. Countering the current hegemony is therefore a pressing challenge for critical pedagogy. Regardless of the nature of its manifestation, Engels (1880/2007) (and Marx) identifies this agent as primarily within those who rely on a wage to survive, the working class, which, from this Marxist conception of social class, is nearly all of humanity, from those whose lives are cut short from the extreme exploitation rampant in so-called Third-World sweat shops to relatively privileged university professors in the so-called First World (despite this great diversity of privilege and suffering within it). Making the point that social change tends to come from social classes that are experiencing unresolvable structural barriers to becoming and who are aware of their own material conditions, using capitalism as an example, Engels (1880/2007) is instructive:

> The new productive forces have already outgrown the capitalist mode of using them. And this conflict between productive forces and modes of production is not a conflict engendered in the mind of man, like that between original sin and divine justice. It exists in fact, objectively, outside us, independently of the will and actions of even the men who brought it on. Modern socialism is nothing but the reflex, in thought, of this conflict in fact; its ideal reflection in the minds, first, of the class directly suffering under it, the working class (p. 73).

This too is where our critical pedagogy should look for a concrete understanding of the world in which we confront. Such insights lead to the conclusion that the only path for humanity to take to save itself is to collectively negate capitalism by negating itself as alienated labor as such. Again, this requires an global antiracist politics that the election of Obama suggests exists as a potential within America. *Race, Power, and the Obama Legacy* offers many insights toward these ends.

References

Engels, F. (2007). *Socialism: Utopian and scientific*. New York: Path Finder. (Original work published 1880)

Harvey, D. (2014). *Seventeen contradictions and the end of capitalism*. New York: Oxford University Press.

Marx, K. (1967). *Capital: A critique of political economy* (Vol. 1). New York: International. (Original work published 1867)

Mészáros, I. (2011). *Social structure and forms of consciousness: Volume II: The dialectic of structure and history*. New York: Monthly Review.

Party for Socialism and Liberation. (2015). *Imperialism in the 21st Century: Updating Lenin's Theory a Century Later* (B. Becker, Ed.). San Francisco, CA: Liberation Media.

1
RACE, POWER, OBAMA'S PRESIDENCY AND LEGACY

What I am finding very disheartening is a rise of blatant expressions of racism, on at least two fronts. First, president Obama is being attacked in ways that I do not recall previous presidents being attacked. There is a mean-spiritedness to many of these attacks, such as comparing him with Hitler, questioning his citizenship, and that kind of thing. And the Republican Party seems to be stoking potential fears that White people have of having a Black person in charge while the nation is experiencing huge economic problems—that was actually leaked as a strategy in a PowerPoint presentation at a Republican strategizing meeting. Second is the number of blatant expressions of racism in society and on college campuses. We are seeing nooses hung, swastikas drawn, and racist epithets hurled at Black students. So, although I would like to think that his election can change perceptions, there is a backlash that is frightening. I don't think just him being elected and becoming president will necessarily change that. It depends on what sorts of policies flow from his election. Look at the recession and what people are dealing with. I am not sure there has necessarily been any improvement in people's conditions of life yet. I hope he is around for eight years so that we can see what happens. But just electing one person to a high office alone does not change things, especially when the policies he tries to advance are attacked as strongly as they are.

(Christine Sleeter, as cited in Orelus, 2011, p. 72)

Introduction

White males have historically dominated the political system of the United States. Therefore, Barack Obama's remarkable ascendency to the presidency is unquestionably a significant shift in the US political paradigm. Because of the magnitude and historic meaning of Obama's victory, there have been many controversial debates about it. Political pundits, social activists, public intellectuals, and ordinary citizens have taken a wide range of positions about Obama's presidency and administration. While well-known political leaders and public intellectuals, such as Reverend Al Sharpton and Michael Eric Dyson, have defended Obama pointing out the historical significance of his political victory and domestic policy favoring women and gay rights, others, like Cornel West, have harshly criticized him, pointing out the flaws of both his domestic and foreign policies. For example, West accused Obama of being "a black mascot of Wall Street oligarchs and a black puppet of corporate plutocrats" (West, as cited in Thompson, 2011, p. 1). Similarly, the world-acclaimed journalist and the founder of WikiLeaks, Julian Assange (2012), called Obama "a wolf in sheep's clothing." Likewise, while talking about President Obama, Oliver Stone (2014), the Academy Award–winning director, stated, "I think that under a disguise of sheep's clothing, he's been a wolf."

To shed light on both criticism and praises made about Obama's presidency and administration, this chapter, aligned with the focus and overarching goals of the book, begins by briefly examining Obama's backgrounds. It further explores the interest convergence factor that has led many White liberals and the corporate media to endorse and strategically help Obama get elected in 2008 and reelected in 2012. By interest convergence, it is meant that both President Obama and those who have supported him, including White liberals and the corporate world, share similar political and socioeconomic interests, among others.

Moreover, this chapter looks at Obama's political accomplishment, including parts of his domestic policy that support gay rights and equal pay for women. In addition, this chapter examines Obama's educational policies, like *Race to the Top*, and the effects of such policies on the learning and academic outcome of students, particularly poor linguistically and culturally diverse students. Furthermore, this chapter points out the effects of Obama's foreign policy on the lives of people in countries like Somalia, Afghanistan, Pakistan, Iraq, and Yemen, where innocent Black and Brown children and women have been killed by drone strikes authorized by the Obama's government. I end this chapter by projecting Obama's legacy drawing on the implementation and effects of his domestic and foreign policies.

Obama: An Account of His Background

The son of a Kenyan immigrant father and a Caucasian American woman, Barack Hussein Obama was raised by his White mother and later by his two White grandparents and an uncle (Obama, 2004). Growing up, Obama was apprenticed into White culture, norms, and values. Such experience has differentiated him in many ways from many African Americans whose parents, grandparents, and great-grandparents were slaves experiencing the savage effects of structural racism and White supremacy in the United States. For example, unlike many African Americans, Obama appears to be quite comfortable being around and interacting with Whites, although in certain political contexts he might have performed whiteness for political survival reasons.

Obama has been able to not only perform whiteness but also to use the White dominant discourse to communicate with the White mainstream. The type of discourse alluded here is the one to which he was exposed at home. Later, through his formal schooling at elitist institutions such as Princeton and Harvard, he was further apprenticed into and acquired White hegemonic discourse and ideology, which he used during electoral campaigns to attract White supporters and voters. These elitist institutions have historically earned the reputation of preparing graduates, particularly White males, for key positions in American society and beyond.

In his adult life, Obama reached out to and built relationships with the African American community and culture, and he has been exposed to and immersed into such community and culture ever since—particularly after marrying his wife, an African American woman. Obama has shown to be quite capable of using his linguistic skills to reach out to African Americans, racially mixed individuals, and Whites, particularly White liberals. Stated otherwise, Obama has used his bicultural and biracial identities to navigate through multiple racial and cultural worlds. He is intellectually and linguistically gifted, as illuminated through his public speeches.

Situating the Context of Obama's Historical Victory

Obama's unique talent as an orator—and his intelligence, pragmatism, and likable personality—must be acknowledged. However, one must go beyond these factors so as to better understand political, socioeconomic, ideological, and racial factors that greatly contributed to Obama's unprecedented historical victory. During the two terms of former US President George W. Bush, the United States endured economic, sociopolitical, and diplomatic agony, both internally and externally. The country had earned a rather negative international reputation for its invasion in and occupation of Afghanistan and Iraq, where cases of tortures of innocent civilians by US soldiers were and continue to be commonplace. Abu Ghraib is a case in point. At this boot camp, US soldiers detained, sexually and physically humiliated, and psychologically tortured innocent Iraqi people by stripping them and beating them like savages.

This human atrocity, committed by US soldiers in Abu Ghraib, exacerbated the political and economic crisis that former President George Bush had already created. To prevent the United States from sinking deeper in the ocean of international shame and isolation, an urgent shift in the US political system had to happen. Internally, the country was (and still is) experiencing socioeconomic, political, and racial unrest, due to the high rate of unemployment, higher cost of living, gender, socioeconomic, racial, and environmental injustices. Given the political, socioeconomic, educational, and racial situations of the country at the time, Obama appeared to be the safest and most pragmatic choice among all the potential candidates. To put it simply, the country needed a candidate and leader like Barack Obama who is biracial and bicultural, endowed with a high intellect, a likable personality, and, most importantly, whose ideology seemingly did not pose a threat or an eminent threat to the White establishment, US capitalism and imperialism.

Obama seemed to have emerged from nowhere. He surfaced into the political scene because he had strong support from both progressive Whites and non-Whites, including the youth who seemingly were (and still are) thirsty for something novel and inspiring expressed through his public speeches. To many of these youth and adults, Obama's candidacy in 2008 seemed to symbolize a renewed hope. This political propaganda was successfully sold to them, although apparently more so in 2008 than in 2012. He received less support from his base in the 2012 election. For example, in the 2008 election, 131 million people voted, and Barack Obama defeated John McCain by a 53 percent to 46 percent margin. By contrast, in 2012 Obama received 65,915,796 popular votes, while his opponent, Mitt Romney, received 60,933,500. Obama defeated Romney by a 51.1 percent to 47.2 percent margin. These facts suggest that during his first term Obama might have caused many youth to become disillusioned and disenchanted.

Indeed, Obama seemed to have emerged from nowhere—although his deeply passionate 2004 speech at the Democratic Convention in Boston, Massachusetts, had already contributed to his political exposure. But was this factor alone sufficient to help Obama get elected as the first African American president four years later? As previously stated, Obama's educational opportunities afforded him entry into two of the country's top Ivy League institutions. Still, was this factor enough to enable him to get elected and reelected in a country like the United States, where White supremacy still reigns and poses a horrific challenge to Native Americans, Blacks, Arabs, Latina/os, Asians, and others labeled as *people of color*? Like Obama, many African Americans, such as W.E.B. du Bois, Cornel West, and Henry Louis Gates Jr., graduated from Ivy League institutions. Obama's Ivy League background alone is insufficient to have helped him become the commander in chief of the most powerful country on earth. The use of the word *powerful* needs to be contextualized here, however. Many Western countries have become militarily, politically, and economically powerful by exploiting and oppressing other countries through unfair trades, invasion and occupation, and the United States is no exception.

Even though Obama won the primary election and received the official endorsement of the Democratic Party thereafter, there was still doubt as to whether he would be able to win the general election and become president. Many attacks by both Republicans and Democrats, like his former contenders John McCain and Hillary Clinton, respectively, aimed at attacking Obama's character and backgrounds. He was and continues to be victim of inaccurate and absurd epithets and labels, like being called a Muslim, a racist, a socialist, seemingly aimed at influencing the general public to revolt against him. Tea party leaders and supporters, for example, called him a Muslim, with the intent of transforming the United States into a socialist country. Other opponents, like the former Republican presidential contender, Newt Gingrich, labeled him a welfare president for allowing temporarily unemployed Americans to receive unemployment benefits. McLaren (2011) observes:

> Since the election of Barack Obama, right-wing pundits have unchained a racist fury across the U.S. mediascape, accusing the president of being "demonstrably a racist," of pandering to people of color, of being a race-baiter, of being the "most racial president," of having appointed a "racist administration," of using a "Black accent" when he addresses groups of African Americans, of preying on "White guilt" and using "racial anxiety" to get himself elected, of "defending racism," and of supporting civil rights groups that are nothing more than "race-baiting poverty pimps" (pp. 97–110).

The mean-spirited, racist, and White supremacist attacks against Barack Obama are not surprising in a country where racist Whites have lynched Blacks as recently as the early 1960s. Other forms of lynching have been redesigned, taking place in many cities since slavery and the Jim Crow era. For example, the execution of the African American male, Troy Davis, was, in my opinion, a legalized form of lynching. Mr. Davis was jailed for more than a decade and executed in 2012 for supposedly shooting a police officer in 1989. Years after his execution, there is still no evidence suggesting that he actually committed this crime. Similar forms of legalized murder of African American males by racist civilians and police officers, like those of Trayvon Martin, Michael Brown, Eric Garner, John Crawford, Ezell Ford, and Dante Parker have occurred in this country since Obama was elected.

The racist attacks against Obama by White supremacist groups are not justifiable. However, it is unrealistic to not expect such attacks to emerge after the country had elected and reelected the first president of color after centuries of White male political domination. This country is still dealing with a past tainted with slavery, colonization, and the Jim Crow era. America has yet to honestly face and heal from a racial scar of the past that still psychologically haunts both Whites and non-Whites. To heal from such a scar, we first and foremost need to talk honestly and genuinely about race. Unfortunately, as former US attorney general, Eric Holder, observed, "Though race-related issues continue to occupy a significant portion of our political discussion, and though there remain many unresolved racial issues in this nation, we, average Americans, simply do not talk enough with each other about race" (Holder, as cited in Early & Kennedy, 2010, p. 224). Unless we genuinely and honestly talk about racism and take actions to combat it, racial tension among Whites and non-Whites would most likely continue to occur. Such tension has rendered more challenging the fight for racial, socioeconomic, and gender justice, peace, and freedom that many social and political activists across race, class, sexuality, and gender have been involved in for decades and for which many have lost their lives.

During the 2008 and 2012 electoral campaigns, Obama faced vicious racist White supremacist attacks. Yet he found inner strength and strategic ways to inspire youth and adults from various sectors in society to vote for him in masses leading to his political victories. Racist attacks and harsh, unfounded forms of criticism from right-wingers against Obama did not deter people from seeing him as a transcending leader—one who has been able to capture the imagination, aspiration, and collective spirit of many Americans, particularly the youth, in both the 2008 and 2012 elections. However, the debatable question still remains: Would Obama have been elected president had both of his parents been African Americans?

Obama Versus Other African Americans

Like most people of color, Obama has certainly experienced racism. However, unlike many African Americans, he did not inherit a family history marked with naked forms of racism, like lynching. Obama has no family members or ancestors being lynched on either side of his parents' history. Therefore, even though Obama is labeled and treated as African American, he might not fully understand how it feels to be a descendant of slaves and treated as such in the "democratic" United States, where White supremacy remains a daily specter haunting descendants of slave ancestors. It is one thing to learn about slavery and lynching in school—often through racially biased textbooks—but it is another to experience them firsthand. To put it simply, theory can't ever replace practice—nor can practice stand on its own without being supported and informed by theory.

By using this metaphor, it is meant to point out that as someone who has no history of slavery in his family, Barack Obama might never fully comprehend the level of anger that the history of slavery and the bloody Jim Crow era have caused African Americans and other Blacks descendant of slave ancestors, and why many of them have reacted differently to White supremacy and institutional racism. Even though Obama has been perceived, labeled, and treated as Black or African American, culturally he still benefits from his biracial identity, shaped mostly by whiteness on his mother's side of the family. This factor alone has differentiated him from many other Africans, African Americans, and Blacks. For example, although Obama's father lived under colonization and experienced its savage effects, Obama himself is not able to draw on personal experience to speak about this painful experience.

Obama barely knew his father. In fact, as he explained it himself in *Dreams from My Father*, he did not meet his father until he was 10 years old, after being abandoned by him when he was only a baby (Obama, 2004). Obama's African roots and biracial identity are complicated but seemed to have worked in his favor while running for president. That is, in the eyes of many people—including White liberals—Obama is a different kind of Black; he is seen as different in many ways from many African American leaders who have preceded him. For example, in private conversations during the 2008 US presidential election, Senate Majority Leader Harry Reid labeled Barack Obama as "light skinned" and "with no Negro dialect." This racially and linguistically biased statement caused much racial controversy among Whites and non-Whites from various ideological and political positions until Obama's political victory in November 2008.

Obama's public discourse and performance of his masculinity tend to be different from those of African American leaders like Jessie Jackson. For instance, Obama's discourse is much closer to White dominant discourse than African American vernacular, although he has proven to be able to code switch and uses both. Were all the linguistic and cultural attributes identified above sufficient to help him get elected? Would Obama have been elected president had he not been a biracial individual with a White identity? These questions have been the center of many heated political debates. Sonia Nieto (2011), a world-leading multicultural education scholar, states,

> Had Obama been only African American rather than biracial, it would have been harder. But he is a different kind of Black leader from the Black leaders we have had in the past, who focused a lot on race. This is just a different time, and you could never be a Black man focusing on race and expect to win the presidency of the United States. You can't be. Maybe in twenty or thirty years you can, who knows? (p. 81)

Nieto's acknowledgement of the advantageous role that Obama's biracial identity played in his magisterial political victory is worth noting. It must also be acknowledged that his political victory has much more to do with his ideology and stance on many socioeconomic and political issues including his ambivalent positions on the war in Afghanistan that he perpetuated and his association with and support for corporate banks that his government bailed out. These politically motivated positions and actions seem to be a manifestation of the color of Obama's ideology, personal and political interests.

Obama Trapped by the White Hegemonic Power Structure: Is His Legacy in Peril?

President Obama is placed within a White power structure historically dominated by conservative White males, mostly Christian, who have for centuries played the hegemonic role serving the US empire. The corporate world and the White power structure within which Obama is leading the United States is an important factor that must be taken into consideration, particularly in the analysis of the short- and long-term consequences of his domestic and foreign policies. Failing to do so would limit any critical analysis of his government.

The US presidency was not designed for a man of Obama's racial background. Instead, it was conceived by and for White males, particularly privileged Christian, heterosexual White males. Hence, how might it feel to be the first African American commander in chief of an imperial and White hegemonic state? Only Obama can answer this question. Only he knows, for example, how it feels to be undermined and called names by conservative Whites, including White males in the US Congress. Due to the social construction of race, which is linked to the lasting legacy of slavery, colonization, and White supremacy, Blacks are represented and treated as less intelligent and less competent than Whites.

It is, therefore, not surprising that Obama's mere presence as a man of color in the White House represents a threat, even though such house was built on the backbones of Blacks, namely enslaved Africans. Moreover, even though Obama is an American, his citizenship has been questioned by right-wing and White supremacist groups. Lastly, unlike his White predecessors, President Obama has been called derogatory names by White groups and individuals, including his political opponents, determined to portray him as the worst US president in history.

Because Obama has been viciously attacked by conservative Whites, it has been challenging, particularly for progressive intellectuals and social activists of color, to critique his government. It is commonly expected of Blacks, including Black intellectuals, to show solidarity with other Blacks. However, Black intellectuals and journalists, such as Cornel West and Tavis Smiley, have transcended this limited view of racial solidarity to challenge Obama. They have criticized his foreign policy, including his authorization of the use of drone strikes on vulnerable people, including Black and Brown people, living abroad. They have also criticized the Obama administration for spying on citizens. As a result, West and Smiley have been criticized by other Black political figures in the African community, like Reverend Al Sharpton who seems to expect West and Smiley to show understanding, support, and even empathy to Obama as the first president of color leading a superpower like the United States—a country with many inherent racial, socioeconomic, and political problems that President Obama has to grapple with and is expected to solve.

My contention is that regardless of a president's racial background, he or she should be held accountable for his or her actions, and Obama should not be exempted. This is to say that failing to challenge and hold Obama accountable for his actions (as we did for the two former presidents George W. Bush and Bill Clinton) might lead one to believe we are racially biased. Challenging and holding Obama's government accountable for unfulfilled promises made and atrocities his government commits against people, particularly the vulnerable, is or should be a moral and political imperative for concerned citizens and true patriots.

Critiquing Obama's domestic and foreign policies and the effects of these policies on the poor does not and should not take anything away from his recognized talent, intelligence, charisma, and political charm, as well as his political courage to publically speak in favor of gay rights and equal pay for women. Nor should critiquing Obama's policies make a person of color a traitor or unpatriotic. Obama must be held accountable for his actions. Race should not be used as an alibi to silence those who have dared critique Obama's policies. One's blind loyalty to an individual pertaining to the same racial group is nothing but *racial fanaticism*. Those adhering to racial fanaticism have yet to think and decide for themselves. Racial fanatics are found in all races, and they tend to be intolerant to different point of views expressed by members of the same racial group.

Whites should not fear being called racist for criticizing Obama for his political decisions and actions, as long as their criticism is not informed by racial hatred stemming from White supremacist ideology and motives. Critiquing Obama's government should be the role and responsibility of all citizens, including teachers, students, social activists, and activist intellectuals, irrespective of their racial, ethnic, linguistic, sexual, and religious backgrounds, and ideological positions. For example, critiquing Obama's domestic policy affecting the most vulnerable groups—the poor, including children of deported mothers or fathers—should be the moral and political duty of all citizens who care for the humanity of others.

It is undeniable that Obama is in a very challenging position as the first African American president of an imperialist, capitalist, and White-dominated country. For example, he has been counseled by many White males who might have much to gain by maintaining the US corporate, capitalist, and imperialist world order. Consequently, Obama might have been forced to make unwise socioeconomic and political decisions affecting the lives of ordinary people. What is more, for the same reason Obama might have been compelled to take political decisions aimed at strengthening the US empire, and refusing to do so might have put his life and that of his family in danger—even though being the first African American president alone has already put him and his family in a perilous predicament.

These examples are used to point out that the perception of people located at the periphery of the political power structure is sharply different from the firsthand experience of those who are operating within such a structure. Obama might have faced many challenges that many of us located outside the power structure might be unaware of. However, while what is argued here may be true, this should not excuse Obama from any criticism regarding his political actions—after all, he is the commander in chief. Specifically, he is the president with much executive power that the constitution allows him to use to protect, for example, the human rights of all people, including those of undocumented individuals immigrating to the United States in search of a better life for themselves and their families. It is disheartening in a self-declared democratic country like the United States that immigrants, particularly immigrants of color, have been treated as the scum of the earth even though their hard and cheap labor has contributed to the economic development as well as cultural, religious, linguistic, and racial diversity of this country. The xenophobic and neoliberal nature of Obama's domestic policy leading to the massive form of deportation of poor immigrants of color needs to be exposed. Likewise, his authorization of the use of drone strikes against innocent people, the implementation of his economic policy that favor the rich over the poor, and the disastrous effects of his educational policy, *Race to the Top*, need to be unpacked.

The Legacy of Obama's Presidency

Unlike many people of color and White allies might have expected, the presidency of Barack Obama has not and most likely will not fundamentally change the socioeconomic, educational, and political conditions of African Americans and other marginalized racial groups. For example, in 2011, two researchers from Economic Policy Institute, Shierholz and Gould, report:

> The black household earning the median income is now bringing in $5,494 less than the median black household did 10 years ago (a drop of 14.6 percent) and the median Hispanic household is now bringing in $4,235 less than the median Hispanic household did 10 years ago (a drop of 10.1 percent) (p. 1).

Shierholz and Gould further note,

> Non-Hispanic whites maintained far lower poverty rates than any other racial/ethnic group. Blacks were particularly hard-hit by increases in poverty from 2009 to 2010, increasing 1.6 percentage points to reach a rate of 27.4 percent. In 2010, over one-third of black children (39.1 percent) and Hispanic children (35.0 percent) were living in poverty. The poverty rate for families with children headed by single mothers hit 40.7 percent in 2010. Of the 7.0 million families living in poverty in 2010, 4.1 million of them were headed by a single mom (p. 3).

As these statistical facts reveal, Blacks and other minoritized groups have experienced more dire economic challenges under President Barack Obama than under his predecessor, George W. Bush, and others. Furthermore, more undocumented immigrants of color have been deported under Obama—not to mention the killing of Black and Brown people in Afghanistan, Pakistan, and Iraq through drone strikes taking place during his presidency. Yet, ironically, this is a president about whom the following reassuring and hopeful comment was made.

The political victory of Barack Obama is an indication that some level of racial progress, though still insignificant, has been made in the United States. Marable states, "For a nation that had, only a half century earlier, refused to enforce the voting rights and constitutional liberties of people of African descent, to elevate a black American as its chief executive, was a stunning reversal of history" (Marable, as cited in Rickford, 2011, p. 232). However, Obama's racial victory does not necessarily guarantee socioeconomic prosperity for racially marginalized groups in the United States, much less elsewhere in the globe. Specifically, his racial victory does not necessarily mean that African Americans and other racially, socioeconomically, and historically marginalized groups are better off. Nor does Obama's political victory mean the end of White supremacy and institutionalized racism. In fact, White supremacist groups, like the tea party, have become more visible publically than ever before. Obama's political victory has been mostly symbolic.

Many political pundits argued that racism is no longer an issue in the United States following the political triumph of Barack Obama. Kennedy (2010) states, "For conservative optimists, Obama's election represents 'mission accomplished.' They point to it as further justification for their claim that it is up to individual blacks to take advantage of opportunities that are now widely available" (p. xx). Kennedy goes further, noting:

> The editorial page of the *Wall Street Journal* voiced this conservative optimism when it declared the day after Obama's election that "perhaps we can put to rest the myth of racism as a barrier to achievement in this splendid country." A respondent to a newspaper articulated the same point more crudely but revealing when he averred: "I don't want to hear any more crap about whites keeping blacks down. A black man in the oval office renders this argument moot" (p. xx).

These statements fail to capture a very important political fact: the political victory of Barack Obama is informed by interest convergence between elite Whites and Obama (Bell, 1980). Elite Whites seem to have much to gain in allowing an African American, who did not and still does not pose a serious threat to their corporate political and economic interests. By saying that President Obama was elected because of interest convergence, it is not intended that his competence and talent be disregarded. Indeed, President Barack Obama is highly educated, very charismatic, and knows how to navigate the White political apparatus to achieve political goals.

As an individual person of color surrounded by Whites, particularly White male politicians and lobbyists who have influenced and controlled the US political system for centuries, Obama could not and would not change this system. Besides, Obama never pretended to be a radical.

Obama has not, and most likely would not (until the end of his second term) take a position that threatens the US capitalist and imperialist system. In fact, since he has been in power, both his domestic and foreign policies have strengthened the US corporate capitalist and imperialist system, favoring the rich and huge corporations over the poor and the marginalized. To put it simply, both Obama's domestic and foreign policies buttress the US capitalist and imperialist system. This is a matter of great educational and political importance that cannot be ignored.

Despite some progressive steps aforementioned taken by his government, Obama must be held accountable for the corporate capitalist and imperialist actions he took against the poor here in this country and abroad. For example, like many of his predecessors, Obama's government has participated in the invasion of many countries—including Libya, leading to the overthrow of the Kaddafi regime. Obama is the first US Black president, yet he contributed to the murder of an African leader and the killing of innocent Africans through drone strikes in countries such as Somalia (Scahill, 2013).

Furthermore, Obama's government defended and continues to defend the National Security Agency's (NSA) spying practices against American citizens and foreign leaders, like Brazilian President Dilma Rousseff and German Chancellor Angela Merkel (Greenwald, 2015). Moreover, Obama has supported authoritarian governments in the Middle East, like the Yemenis and Egyptian governments, which have tortured innocent civilians and opponents (Greenwald, 2013; Scahill, 2013). Equally worse, Obama's government has committed repugnant crimes against humanity by detaining and torturing innocent people in Guantanamo Bay prison (Greenwald, 2015). Finally, although in his public speeches he pretends to be fighting for the so-called middle class, his actions and policies have served mainly the corporate interests of the rich at the expense of the poor, as Smiley and West (2012) have eloquently illuminated in their book, *The Rich and the Rest of Us*.

In many communities, including communities of color, Obama's controversial domestic and foreign policies have caused many heated debates and much division among many leaders and public intellectuals, like Al Sharpton and Eric Dyson, who have supported Obama's government. By contrast, Cornel West, Harry Belafonte, and Danny Glover, among others, have criticized Obama's imperialist actions against Third World peoples, including his authorization of the use of drone strikes, leading to the death of innocent people in Yemen, Afghanistan, Pakistan, and Somalia. These highly respected African American intellectuals and activists have also criticized Obama for his economic policy, which seems to favor the rich over the poor. In addition, Obama has been harshly criticized for his draconian immigration policy that has led to the deportation of millions of undocumented immigrants, particularly immigrants of color.

Research demonstrates that under Obama the US government has deported more immigrants than any previous government (Chomsky, 2014). Specifically, since Obama has been in power, millions of immigrants have been deported, whereas others, including children, are incarcerated facing deportation and/or have been deported without due legal process. Furthermore, although he is a constitutional lawyer by training, Obama ordered the unlawful killing of innocent people, like American-born cleric Anwar al-Awlaki and his Denver-born 16-year-old son, Abdulrahman. These two individuals and Samir Khan, all murdered in Yemen, were never charged with a crime.

Finally, Obama's educational policy has been detrimental to students' academic achievement (Giroux, 2008, 2010). Some of his educational policies, like *Race to the Top*, influence the academic outcome of many students negatively, including students of color and poor Whites, perpetuating the academic gap that has long existed between affluent and poor students (Carr & Portfilio, 2011). For example, like the *No Child Left Behind* mandate, *Race to the Top*'s implementation has reduced teachers' practices to preparing underprivileged students attending public schools for standardized tests (Giroux, 2010). These students are required to take these tests in order to be allowed to move from one grade to another, or to graduate. By contrast, students from affluent families go to private schools where they are not expected to take state and federal mandated standardized tests that are hypothetically aimed at measuring their growth and academic success (Darder, 2012). Nor are they punished for failing these standardized tests, which are often culturally and racially and class based.

In matters of race, Obama's public speeches do not seem to pose a threat to Whites, particularly White liberals. For instance, his few public speeches on race have never brought to the fore issues of White supremacy and structural racism. As will be further discussed in the book, Obama's speech on race seems to be consistently confined within the safe zone, seemingly because of his fear of upsetting Whites, both liberal and conservative. His very few speeches on this topic have been caused by unprecedented and brutal murder cases, like that of Trayvon Martin. One therefore must ask: Had it not been for this highly publicized murder case, which compelled him to make a public statement (for which he was harshly criticized by right-wing Republicans like Newt Gingrich, who accused him of racializing this murder) would President Barack Obama have taken a stance on racial issues in this country? Race talk is something that must be avoided as much as possible, and Obama understood this well early on in his political career. He never mentioned race in his campaign speeches until he was forced to do so to appease the political tension caused by his association with Reverend Jeremiah Wright, who has been very critical of US domestic and foreign policies, including racially biased policies affecting African Americans and people of color in general.

White supremacy and structural racism in this country persist, and continue to be one of the root causes of the impoverishment of African Americans, Native Americans, Latino/as, Blacks, Asians, immigrants of color, and other oppressed groups (Bonilla-Silva, 2010). Yet, the postracial discourse, emerging after Barack Obama was elected and reelected as the first Black president in the United States in 2008 and 2012, respectively, prevails in the mainstream media. It seems this discourse, circulated and sold to the public, has been used as an ideological mechanism to mask increasing savage racial, socioeconomic, and educational inequalities facing people of color (Kozol, 1992, 2006).

In the beginning, Obama's political victory gave hope to many people of color and progressive Whites. Unfortunately, to many racially marginalized groups and Whites who supported him, such hope diminished after his election in 2008 and reelection in 2012. Domestically, racial, socioeconomic, and educational conditions of African Americans, Native Americans, Latino/as, Asians, and immigrants of color have not improved much, if at all, with either of Obama's elections to the presidency. Yet symbolically his presidency continues to be used as a political alibi by right-wingers, including White supremacist groups, to terrorize historically oppressed groups by blaming them for their lack of success in this "democratic land" of the free. To put it simply, Obama's political victory has been strategically used by the White oligarchic, supremacist establishment to cover up the racial and socioeconomic apartheid in the United States that historically racialized groups have faced in the US society and beyond. The United States has earned a negative reputation worldwide for its racism, including the forcible placement of Native Americans in boarding schools, the Japanese in internment camps, and the enslavement of Blacks, specifically African Americans. The United States is also known for its imperialist invasion, occupation, and economic and political exploitation of underdeveloping countries like Mexico, Panama, Haiti, the Dominican Republic, Grenada (Acuna, 2014; Zinn, 2001), and recently Afghanistan and Iraq.

Despite the high level of emotion that Obama's victory stirred up in the psyche of many communities of color in the United States and disfranchised communities of color around the world, his victory remains a historical and political symbol. Obama has continued the brutal, discriminatory, capitalist, and imperialist practices of his predecessors, like George W. Bush. Specifically, like his predecessors, Obama has proven to be an imperialist, war president, and he has aligned himself with the corporate world at the expense of the poor—a word he hardly used in his public speeches (Galston, 2010).

Obama often uses the middle-class discourse when referring to Americans who are struggling financially as a result of governmental corruption and corporate-based economic policy and regulations. The situation he describes concerning the so-called middle class does not reflect the daily economic and racial reality of the poor. President Obama's middle-class discourse implies that the United States is divided between super rich and the middle class. The poor are not included in his hegemonic political discourse. This clearly shows that Obama's stance on class issue influences his political decisions—while at the same time unveiling his limited view and understanding of this issue. Moreover, under Obama's administration, innocent people continue to be unfairly incarcerated and inhumanly treated in Guantanamo Bay prison, contradicting his electoral promise to close this racist boot camp. In short, the presidency of Barack Obama has been used as a green light by the White supremacist establishment to continue to conceal poverty in the United States and the ongoing racial discrimination against Native Americans, African Americans, Blacks, Latina/o s, Asians, immigrants of color, Arabs, and other marginalized groups.

There are numerous scholars who have scrutinized Obama's domestic and foreign policies. For example, in *Politics After Hope*, Giroux (2010) critically examines Obama's politics of hope, arguing that such politics gradually has been changed into a politics of accommodation and deceit. Specifically, Giroux's contention is that to many of Obama's supporters, his administration has been a deception, and he points out racial and socioeconomic injustices and assault on democracy repeatedly since Obama was elected. Equally significant, Giroux challenges Obama's administration, stating that policies grounded in ethics of hope, civic responsibilities, and profound educational changes are sine qua non conditions for a true participatory democratic society.

Similarly, in *The People vs. Barack Obama*, Shapiro (2014) provides a sharp critique of President Obama by unveiling the abuses committed by his administration, from the US Department of Justice to the National Security Agency, and from the Environmental Protection Agency to the Department of Health and Human Services. Shapiro contends that Barack Obama's administration has increasingly become a web of dishonesty, bribery, and corruption impacting nearly all aspects of Americans' lives. In specific terms, Shapiro maintains that Obama's government has been transformed into a political machine that spies on civilians violating their rights, that micromanages the economy, that enforces immigration laws leading to the deportation of countless undocumented immigrants, and that violates the constitution when it is convenient to do so for the maintenance of his presidency.

Finally, in *The Phenomenon of Obama and the Agenda for Education*, Carr and Portfilio (2011) critically examine Obama's neoliberal policies, illuminating ways and the degree to which such policies have impacted the teaching practices of teachers working particularly with poor, historically marginalized students as well as the learning outcome of these students. Carr and Portfilio, and contributors to their edited volume, invite policy makers, educators, and citizens concerned with the future of education and its direct relation to participatory democratic society to be vigilant, to challenge and hold Obama's administration accountable for his neoliberal policies affecting the learning of students through the mandates of his educational policies such as *Race to the Top*, which is in essence a replication of the *No Child Left Behind* mandate.

Obama's presidency is complex and his legacy will be controversial. Some of the major domestic and foreign policy decisions and political events that would shape Obama's legacy include:

1. His public support of gay and women's rights. Obama deserves much credit for standing up for these groups that have been historically marginalized and oppressed in society. Queer folks and women have been discriminated against, underpaid, unappreciated, and psychologically and physically abused by the patriarchal system. Queer folks have not only been discriminated at work and in school, but also have been denied equal right to get married, and many have been murdered simply for being different. Obama's stance on women's equal rights is to be commended as well.

2. Obama will be remembered for attempting to resume and normalize US diplomatic relations with Cuba. For over 50 years, the United States has imposed an embargo on the socialist Cuban regime following the 1959 revolution leading to the departure of the Cuban dictator, Baptista. Since this revolution, these two countries have been involved in unresolved political, ideological, and political conflicts.

3. His legacy will also be marked by his authorized assassination of Osama Bin Laden, which made him even more popular worldwide.

This assassination generated and continues to generate political and legal controversy due to the way that Obama's government killed bin Laden. World political critics and analysts, such as Noam Chomsky, argue that Obama's government violated Bin Laden's human rights by killing him in the way that it did. According to Chomsky and other critics, Obama's government could have captured Bin Laden and brought him to justice (as he was accused of being an international criminal) but they chose not to do so. He was killed with impunity and his body thrown into the sea as if he had no human right to be brought to justice for the crime he was accused of committing against humanity. Conversely, those who supported and celebrated Obama's decision to kill Bin Laden saw the latter as an international criminal who deserved to be physically erased from this planet by any means.

4. Obama's legacy will be blemished, however, by his authorization to kill innocent people through drone strikes as well as by his political decision to spy on citizens here in the United States and abroad.

5. Obama's legacy will also be tainted by his support of oppressive governments like Yemen, which has murdered its citizens, and the Israeli government that has been occupying and oppressing the Palestinian people. For example, during the Israeli invasion of Gaza in 2014 that led to the murder of nearly 200,000 Palestinians (mostly civilians and including innocent babies and children) and the massive destruction of houses, schools, and hospitals, Obama stated publicly that Israel has the right to defend itself against Hamas. Obama was right: Israel does have a right to defend itself against Hamas, like any other country. But how about Palestinians? Do not they have the right to defend themselves as well? Unfortunately, Obama's public support for the Israeli government only gave Israel the green light to continue its genocide with impunity against the Palestinian people.

6. Finally, Obama's legacy will be impacted by his decision to bail out corporate banks that have exploited and further impoverished poor and working-class people through subprime loans.

Outline of Chapters

Chapter two examines (1) whether or not with Obama's political victory, fundamental change is or was possible within the existing sociopolitical structures of a White capitalist and supremacist system and (2) to what extent his presidency might have been utilized as a political symbol to mask the ongoing misery of poor people of color, poor Whites, and other marginalized groups. I begin by critically examining two major oppressive systems, racism and capitalism. The actions undertaken by the architects of these systems have impacted poor, marginalized people, and most likely will continue to impact people's lives. Furthermore, I explore the extent to which Obama's political decision to appoint many conservative White males in his administration might have reflected the type of change he talked about through his campaign. Finally, I analyze some of President Barack Obama's political speeches, examining the manner in which the content of these speeches points to educational, racial, socioeconomic, and political challenges facing oppressed groups. Yet Obama has not and most likely would not do much to improve these conditions.

Chapter three explores the intersection between Black masculinity, institutionalized racism, patriarchy, and White supremacy. The chapter begins with a critical analysis of the manner in which many privileged White males, like US Vice President Joe Biden, have labeled some men of color, like Obama, "clean and articulate" to promote them at the expense of those who dare challenge the White status quo. Moreover, this chapter examines the hegemonic discourse of blaming the "other," showing how this discourse has failed to capture the underlying reasons that have prevented many marginalized men of African descent from providing for and being involved in the lives of their families. Last, this chapter illuminates how Black masculinity has been colored by institutionalized racism, White patriarchy, and White supremacy. It goes on to demonstrate ways and the degree to which men of color, including Barack Obama, have been misrepresented in the media. President Obama is used as the prime example to point out how classism, elitism, and heterosexism complicate Black masculinity.

The fourth chapter examines ways and the extent to which internalized oppression has influenced the behavior and actions of many people of color, including political leaders like President Barack Obama. Specifically, this chapter argues that because of internalized oppression and the legacy of White supremacy and colonization, many leaders of color acceding to political power after centuries of White male political dominance have engaged in abusive practices similar to those committed by their White male predecessors. President Obama along with three African leaders—namely Joseph Mugabe, Mobuto Sese Seko, and Blaise Compaoré—as prime examples, are used as cases in point to show the manner in which they have reproduced similar abusive, authoritarian, imperialist actions as those of their White male predecessors.

Using the racial controversy in which President Obama, Professor Henry Louis Gates, Jr., and Sergeant James Crowley were involved in 2009 as a building block, chapter five analyzes how White hegemony has led to the silencing of race and its effects on the lives of those who have been racially profiled and historically marginalized, like Black and Brown men and women. Further, this chapter unveils the racial and sociopolitical nature of the controversy. Finally, suggestions are made as to how genuine racial harmony among Whites and non-Whites can be nourished and promoted.

Through an engaged conversation, in chapter six, Professors Bonilla-Silva and Orelus discuss Obama's stance on race, class, and gender issues. They concur that Obama's presidency will not lead to the betterment of socioeconomic conditions of poor Black and Brown people, as many might have hoped. For example, throughout the conversation Professor Bonilla-Silva states that Obama will be "a symbol for White people." The authors' analysis is not limited to Obama's presidency. Throughout this chapter, Professor Bonilla-Silva and Orelus critically examine the harmful effects of racism, sexism, classism, and homophobia on poor Black, White, Latino/as, and queer folks.

Drawing on the current socioeconomic and political situations of Third World countries—including Palestine, Afghanistan, and Haiti—chapter seven demonstrates through concrete examples how Obama's foreign policy is not so different from that of his White male predecessors. Like the White male presidents who preceded him, Obama uses an imperial discourse when referring to currently invaded and occupied countries such as Afghanistan and Iraq. This chapter further argues that since Obama came to power, there has not been a significant shift in US foreign policy vis-à-vis countries labeled as "Third World." Under his command, the United States continues with its imperialist and neo-liberal policy abroad. Iraq and Afghanistan are still occupied by US imperialist armed forces, and innocent civilians, including students, continue to lose their lives through drone strikes.

Conclusion

Like many books written on Obama's presidency and legacy, including the ones briefly reviewed in this chapter, this book critically examines the success—however small it might have been in the eyes of educators, political analysts, and concerned citizens—and shortcomings of Obama's administration by critically analyzing and situating both his domestic and foreign policies in specific political, socioeconomical, racial, and ideological context. Specifically, this book unveils short- and long-term effects of both his domestic and foreign policies, pointing out the ways and the degree to which such policies have benefited certain groups and corporations in American society while at the same time impacting the socioeconomic and political lives of ordinary people, particularly those of the poor here and abroad. This book aims to create political awareness about the implications of Obama's presidency and legacy for people, particularly people of color and poor Whites.

2
OBAMA DANCING WITH VOUCHER CAPITALISM AND WHITE HEGEMONY

I don't think we are in kind of post-racial period. Racism is certainly alive. The president himself is experiencing that right now in terms of the attacks that have been launched against him. At the same time, there is a quantitative change now. When you have a Black president, it also suggests that there is a much greater number of people in this country that accept the idea of having a Black person in a leadership position. It is not only that we have a Black governor in Massachusetts and a Black governor in New York. We have several icons, from Oprah Winfrey to Michael Jackson, who have crossed borders. There has been a change in racial attitudes, but that doesn't mean we are in a post-racial era.

(Pedro Noguera, as cited in Orelus, 2011, p. 164)

Obama is a black mascot of Wall Street oligarchs and a black puppet of corporate plutocrats. And now he has become head of the American killing machine and is proud of it.

(Cornel West, as cited in Thompson, 2011, p.1)

Rich, heterosexual, Christian, capitalist, and conservative White males have monopolized the US political system for centuries. Hence, Barack Obama's historic presidency is undeniably a shift in the US political landscape. In light of this view, this chapter examines Obama's presidency, situating it in the context of US voucher capitalism and White hegemony. Admittedly, not many people of color have been able to emerge from the shadow of the White supremacist and capitalist structure of the United States to become successful politically or otherwise. President Barack Obama is indisputably one of the few. For ordinary poor Black and Brown people who live in disfranchised and racially segregated communities, who have attended poorly funded schools, and who have faced dire socioeconomic, political, and legal challenges, fundamentally nothing much has changed.

As people continue to celebrate Obama's singular political victory, millions of people of color are disproportionately unemployed and facing foreclosure on their homes. According to a report released in 2009 by National League Urban Institute, "Unemployment increased for all groups, but continues to impact blacks and Latinos the most. Whites saw their unemployment increase 0.4% to 7.3%, blacks 0.8% to 13.4% and Latinos saw their unemployment rate increase 1.2% to 10.9%" (p. 2).

It is no coincidence that most people who are unemployed and facing foreclosure are Black and Brown people; race plays a role in the distribution of income and wealth in all forms of societies, particularly in capitalist societies. Some of the negative consequences of the social construction of race include socioeconomic segregation. Childs (2005) argues, "So long as we live in segregated neighborhoods, attend segregated schools, and choose same-race marriage and family, race will be significant social boundary. It is not until we accept race as a social and political construction that affects everyone in society will whites and blacks see themselves as part of the same group" (p. 184).

Since the *Brown v. Board of Education* decision in 1954, intended to desegregate schools, racial segregation in schools has resurfaced in most US cities (Kozol, 2006; Tatum, 2007). Blacks, Latino/as, Native Americans, and Whites continue to attend for the most part "White" and "Black/Brown schools" (Anyon, 1997; Brown et al., 2003; Kozol, 1992, 2006; Tatum, 2003, 2007;) and live in their respective neighborhoods (Bonilla-Silva, 2010; Logan, 2002; Massey & Denton, 1993; Winant, 2001).

Racial segregation in schools is a crucial issue that needs to be brought to the fore of debates revolved around social justice issues (Nieto, 2004; Tatum, 2007). Being embedded in the fabric of the US society, racial segregation has also been the root cause of educational and socioeconomic problems that people of color have faced (Brown et al., 2003; Dyson, 2004; Massey & Denton, 1993; Tatum, 2007; Winant, 2001). Massey and Denton (1993) state:

> Because of racial segregation, a significant share of black America is condemned to experience a social environment where poverty and joblessness are the norm, where a majority of children are born out of wedlock, where most families are on welfare, where educational failure prevails, and where social and physical deterioration abound. Through prolonged exposure to such an environment, black chances for social and economic success are drastically reduced (p. 2).

In the remainder of this chapter, I further explore these issues, situating them in the context of Obama's political victory. Specifically, I examine (1) whether or not fundamental change is possible with Obama's government and (2) to what extent Obama's political victory might have been utilized as a political symbol to mask the ongoing misery of poor people, including racially marginalized groups. I begin by critically examining the two major oppressive systems—racism and capitalism—and showing how these systems would most likely continue to impact poor, marginalized people of color, regardless of Obama's ascendance to the presidency. Furthermore, I look at ways and the extent to which Obama's political decision to appoint many conservatives in his administration reflects the type of change he talked about throughout his campaign. Moreover, I analyze some of his political speeches, pointing out the manner in which he fails to critically address educational, racial, and socioeconomic challenges facing people of color and other oppressed groups. I end this chapter by making an appeal to concerned citizens to organize through grassroots and progressive sociopolitical movements to continuously make President Barack Obama accountable for his promises.

Racism and Voucher Capitalism: Twins of Inequity

Subordination and exploitation of people of color and other oppressed groups do not happen in a vacuum; this subordination and exploitation has been orchestrated through two interlocked oppressive systems, voucher capitalism and racism (Callinicos, 1993; Williams, 1966). Just as the voucher capitalist system cannot survive without oppressing workers (Anyon, 2005; Apple, 2001; Hill, 2001, 2002, 2004; Cole, 2009; Malott, 2013; McLaren, 2005), the racist system that sustains White supremacy cannot survive without brutalizing people of color (Bonilla-Silva, 2003; Brown et al., 2003; Fanon, 1967; Mills, 1997).

Like voucher capitalism, racism is primarily based on profits. In fact, it is a social and historical construct conceived and established by White supremacist groups to exploit and oppress people of color (Baron, 1982; Bell, 1976, 1992, 2004; Bonilla-Silva, 2003; Brown et al., 2003; Cesaire, 2000; Winant, 2001). Here I am not referring to individual racism—that is, the form of racism that a person of color might experience while interacting with an individual White person, or while shopping at a store. Rather, I am referring to *institutionalized* racism, which is often subtle but which has effects that are far more destructive than individual racism (Bonilla-Silva, 2003, 2010; Brown et al., 2003; Fredrickson, 2002; Jensen, 2004; Winant, 2001). For instance, the racism that people of color encounter in their search for housing and employment, in job promotions, and in college admission is a form of institutionalized racism. Specifically, an employer denying a qualified person based on his or her skin color is a form of institutionalized racism. In addition, granting many people of color the worst mortgage loans based on their racial background constitutes a form of institutionalized racism.

Many scholars have explored various and vicious ways institutionalized racism has negatively impacted people of color (Brown et al., 2003; Bonilla-Silva, 2010; Winant, 2001). Brown et al., (2003) maintains, "While young African American men may have the opportunity to obtain the same education, income, and wealth as Whites, in actuality, they are on a slippery slope, for the discrimination their parents faced in the housing and credit markets sets the stage for perpetual economic disadvantage" (p. 21). Similarly, Austin (2009) argues, "The disparities among the college-educated and other evidence strongly suggest that even if the black educational attainment distribution was exactly the same as the white distribution, blacks would still have a higher unemployment rate than whites. Without a renewed commitment to anti-discrimination in employment and job creation in black communities, high rates of black joblessness will likely persist" (p. 1).

Racism is one of the root causes of human tragedy and the source of much the social, economic, and political misery that people of color and other marginalized groups have experienced. The negative effect of racism on people of color and other suppressed groups needs to be critically analyzed and made known to students, but canonical textbooks would not help much because they were and still are mostly written by conservative privileged White males (Apple, 2000, 2003; Kincheloe & Semali, 1999; Lipman, 1998; Loewen, 1995). Furthermore, many privileged and educated people of color who have been used as tokens by the US capitalist and racist systems might not help much, for they might be reluctant to say anything that could endanger their privileged position in the White world. As West (1993) states, "only certain kinds of black people deserve high positions, that is, those who accept the rules of the game played by white America" (p. 42).

Obama Trapped at the Intersection of US Voucher Capitalism and White Supremacy

As the most politically powerful person in the United States, Obama has not overtly spoken against the injustices of the racist and the voucher capitalist systems, fearing doing so might jeopardize his political career, even though he is toward the end of his presidency. His legacy would be marked by his silence about and refusal to speak against these two alienating, oppressive, and inhumane systems. Racism cannot truly be understood without having a clear understanding of how voucher capitalism operates, to which it is linked (Anyon, 2005; Baron, 1982; Callinicos, 1993; Hill, 2001; McLaren, 2005; McLaren & Farahmandpur, 2001; Kelley, 1994; Williams, 1966). Dominant racist groups have used racism as an ideological tool to justify the economic exploitation of people of color. These groups have rendered alienation, oppression, and famine the socioeconomic plight of people of color.

Unlike many privileged Whites, poor people of color and other marginalized groups have been victimized by both the voucher capitalist and racist systems. The root causes of the inhumane plight of Black and

Brown people lies in the structure of a capitalist system that uses racism as its spinal column to make higher profits. Although capitalism is not always a racially based system, in countries such as the United States, capitalism is paired with racism to maintain the unequal distribution of wealth and power of which Black and Brown people are the main victims. Ladner (1998) sheds light on this issue, stating:

> Throughout its history, White America adjusts its expression of racism to accord with its economic imperatives and modifies its myths of racism to take into account the shifting economic circumstances. That is to say, racism remains a persistent value expression depending upon economic opportunities; White America generates a new ideology to sanction any fundamental alterations in race relations growing out of basic economic modifications (pp. 154–155).

For example, while African Americans constitute approximately 15 percent of the US population, the level of poverty among them is higher than any other ethnic group (Anyon, 2005; Bonilla-Silva, 2003, 2010). Bonilla-Silva (2003) states, "Blacks and dark-skinned racial minorities lag well behind whites in virtually every area of social life; they are about three times more likely to be poor than whites, earn about a tenth of the net worth that whites have" (p. 2). African Americans and other Blacks have contributed to the socioeconomic and political advancement of this country. While many serve in the army, or are public school teachers, college professors, lawyers or doctors, others are blue-collar workers working in factories, Burger Kings, and McDonalds. Still, others are selling their labor while being incarcerated (Anyon, 2005; Muhammad, 2008). As Muhammad (2008) states, "Inmates produce items or perform services for almost every major industry. They sew clothes, fight fires and build furniture, but they are paid little or no wages, somewhere between five cents and almost $2" (p. 1).

For many, the so-called American dream remains a dream that might not ever come true. Malcolm X (1965) states, "I'm speaking as a victim of this American system. And I see America through the eyes of the victim. I don't see any American dream; I see an American nightmare" (cited in Marable, 2003, p. 429). Malcolm X's observation is still relevant today as it pointedly speaks to the current social and economic realities of many Black/Brown people. For example, Austin (2009) reports,

> Fifteen months into a deep recession, college-educated white workers still had a relatively low unemployment rate of 3.8% in March of this year. The same could not be said for African Americans with four-year degrees. The March 2009 unemployment rate for college-educated blacks was 7.2%—almost twice as high as the white rate—and up 4.5 percentage points from March 2007, before the start of the current recession (see chart). Hispanics and Asian Americans with college degrees were in between, both with March 2009 unemployment rates of 5% (p. 4).

Even though Americans elected President Barack Obama after more than 200 years of White male political domination, African Americans and other Blacks continue to be disproportionally economically marginalized. Further, the presidency of Barack Obama has not changed their socioeconomic, educational, and political conditions. Blacks and other minoritized groups have experienced more dire economic challenges under Obama than under his predecessor George W. Bush and previous presidents. Finally, more undocumented immigrants of color have been deported under Obama (Hinojosa, 2011), not to mention the killing of Black and Brown people in Afghanistan, Pakistan, and Iraq that continues to take place under his presidency.

Deconstructing Obama's Political Rhetoric

Politically, Barack Obama became nationally visible when he addressed the nation at the 2004 Democratic National Convention taking place in Boston, Massachusetts. In the speech that Obama delivered at this convention, he stated:

> Now even as we speak, there are those who are preparing to divide us, the spin masters and negative ad peddlers who embrace the politics of anything goes. Well, I say to them tonight, there's not a liberal America and a conservative America; there's the United States of America. There's not a black America and white America and Latino America and Asian America; there's the United States of America (Obama, 2004b, p. 2).

This excerpt from that speech does not seem to pose much of a threat to White supremacy. Specifically, the language that he used does not appear to constitute a threat to the hegemonic interests of White conservative groups. President Obama knows that there is a Black, White, Asian, Latino/a, Native American America. This is a reality that should not be denied. Attempting to put race under a beautiful political rug will not help us as a people to move forward.

Had Barack Obama used the rhetoric of, say, Reverend Jeremiah Wright, at the Democratic National Convention in 2004 and during the presidential campaign, most likely he would have been forced out of the presidential race. Obama would have been harshly criticized, as was Reverend Jeremiah Wright, who dared speak against the status quo.

After being attacked by the mainstream media and many White conservative groups for being associated with Reverend Wright, Obama was forced to address the nation about the race issue through a speech he delivered on March 18, 2008 in Philadelphia. In that speech, Obama stated:

> We do need to remind ourselves that so many of the disparities that exist in the African-American community today can be directly traced to inequalities passed on from an earlier generation that suffered under the brutal legacy of slavery and Jim Crow. Segregated schools were, and are, inferior schools; we still haven't fixed them, fifty years after Brown v. Board of Education, and the inferior education they provided, then and now, helps explain the pervasive achievement gap between today's black and white students. Legalized discrimination—where blacks were prevented, often through violence, from owning property, or loans were not granted to African-American business owners, or black homeowners could not access FHA mortgages, or blacks were excluded from unions, or the police force, or fire departments—meant that black families could not amass any meaningful wealth to bequeath to future generations. That history helps explain the wealth and income gap between black and white, and the concentrated pockets of poverty that persists in so many of today's urban and rural communities. A lack of economic opportunity among black men, and the shame and frustration that came from not being able to provide for one's family, contributed to the erosion of black families—a problem that

welfare policies for many years may have worsened. And the lack of basic services in so many urban black neighborhoods—parks for kids to play in, police walking the beat, regular garbage pick-up and building code enforcement—all helped create a cycle of violence, blight and neglect that continue to haunt us (Obama, as cited in Early & Kennedy, 2010, p. 8).

The excerpt of this speech speaks to the socioeconomic injustice that Reverend Wright, many Black leaders such as Martin Luther King, and ordinary people of color have suffered from in this country for centuries. However, being influenced by propaganda circulated through the corporate mass media and being fearful that he might be perceived as just one of those "angry" Black men, Obama found a strategic way to appease the racial tension that Reverend Wright's comments triggered. The political challenge for Obama was to maintain a philosophical solidarity with Reverend Wright and other antiracist theorists and activists while at the same time crafting a political rhetoric that "would do," as he seemed to fear that Reverend Wright's comments would make it challenging for him to continue with the unity and hope messages that he wanted to carry throughout his presidential campaign. One of the tactical ways whereby Obama was able to calm this divided nation was to reassure conservative White folks that he did not share the radical view of his former spiritual mentor. Obama, who was compelled to show to the American White audience that he dissociated himself from Reverend Wright, said in the same speech that:

> Reverend Wright's comments were not only wrong but divisive, divisive at a time when we need unity; racially charged at a time when we need to come together to solve a set of monumental problems—two wars, a terrorist threat, a falling economy, a chronic health care crisis and potentially devastating climate change; problems that are neither black or white or Latino or Asian, but rather problems that confront us all (Obama, as cited in Early & Kennedy, 2010, p. 5).

Even though Obama's speech addresses some of the social, economic, educational, and political inequalities that people of color have suffered for decades in this country, it appears that it was essentially designed to appease the White conservative and White supremacy groups who were infuriated by Reverend Wright's comments. These groups (who are dominated by conservative White males) often feel uneasy about any person of color who dares to challenge a racist and capitalist system that has served their interests for centuries. During the presidential campaign, the mainstream media portrayed Obama as a civil and good man and Reverend Wright as an angry Black man who hates Whites.

This form of ideological discourse can be traced to slavery where slaves who were not perceived as a threat to, or who chose not to challenge White supremacy, were used as tokens by the White masters to demonize and punish other slaves who dared do so. The White practice of tokenizing people of color in this country is not new—the election of Obama may be read as a possible case of tokenizing in that his political rhetoric both draws strength from and at the same time seemingly refutes the racially motivated lived experience of poor people of color. This is an example of the ways in which Obama both seeks nomination, is nominated, and wins the US general election to become the first biracial president. As previously noted, Obama's long apprenticeship into the White dominant discourse has helped him politically in this regard. This apprenticeship has enabled him to speak back to the White world in way that does not seem to be threatening. In short, although Obama's biracial identity is an inescapable and visible marker, his ideological and political performance and charisma have enabled him to rally middle-class and poor working-class White men and women.

Obama's Interest Convergent Victory: A Sign of Racial Unity Among Whites and Non-Whites?

During the 2008 electoral campaign, Obama's ability to rally a plethora of people of mixed race and White people behind his campaign might have led one to believe that, if elected, he would potentially be able to bridge the racial divide and unite the nation. Instead, Obama's historic victory has unfortunately increased the White backlash in this country. Further, his political success story has been appropriated and used by right-wing groups to blame poor people of color and other oppressed people for their lack of success and their abject poverty. People of color are all to be blamed for their own victimization (Ryan, 1976).

Historically, autocratic, conservative, privileged groups are notorious for drawing on the success stories of a few people of color to blame those who have not achieved much by accusing them of being lazy, deficient, and socially unfit. Moreover, Obama's presidency has not stopped privileged White males from running the US political machine. These privileged White males might have decided to endorse Barack Obama because they realized that they could not stop a persistent, charismatic, and an extremely intelligent biracial man. Had President Obama been a mediocre political figure like his predecessor George W. Bush, most likely his Black identity would have been associated with it, and most likely he would not have been elected president.

Many conservative and privileged White male appointees in Obama's administration do not seem to have the political will to help him change the racist and capitalist systems that have been oppressive to poor, Black, Brown, and White people. These conservative and privileged White males have yet to show a genuine interest in alleviating the horrible economic, educational, social conditions of poor people.

Unlike many previous and current political leaders of color, Obama has managed to succeed politically. Indeed, Obama has gone beyond male leaders of color who preceded him in that he has been able to perform the role of president the manner in which many privileged White males have performed it. Unlike his predecessors, through lofty political rhetoric, he was able to do so by using (among other things) his biracial identity to reach out to Blacks, Whites, and people of mixed race. Furthermore, Obama has used throughout his speeches a language that does not appear to challenge the long-established White status quo. Finally, he has performed a type of masculinity that does not seem to be threatening. Therefore, Obama has been intelligently able to navigate through two worlds: the White world and that of people of color. Because of this, he has not only impacted the United States but also the world—all for his own political gains and interests.

However, Obama's political victory has not prevented conservative privileged White males from influencing and profiting from the political apparatus of this country at the expense of the poor. Hence, while celebrating Obama's victory, it is imperative that we incorporate into our analysis race, gender, language, social class, and sexuality, and look at their impact on the political, educational, and economic conditions of people of color and poor Whites. To do otherwise is to deny that poor, historically marginalized groups have been victims both of voucher capitalism, racism, sexism, and homophobia, among other forms of oppression.

Obama's White Political Supporters and Appointees and His Legacy

Obama's access to the country's highest political post is historically unparalleled, However, the socioeconomic, educational, and political conditions of poor Black, Native Americans, Latino/as, Asians, and poor Whites fundamentally remain the same. Moreover, the race relations between people of color and Whites have not improved. It is unlikely President Barack Obama's legacy would profoundly influence the US racial, political, and socioeconomic landscape for the following reason: conservative and privileged White males, who have controlled the wealth of this country for centuries by exploiting marginalized groups through corporate industries and business, dominate the ideological and political club to which Obama currently belongs. Therefore, by association Obama politically reflects the hegemonic interests of these White males. This became more evident during the Democratic National Convention in August 2008. At this convention, both conservative and so-called liberal privileged White men and women stood on the podium and spoke "with pride" about Obama, whom they claimed they endorsed because he represented the interest of every American.

Would they have supported Obama had he unequivocally represented the interests of every American, particularly those of the marginalized? When in American politics have we ever had a candidate or a political leader who truthfully championed and represented the interests of the have-nots while embraced by conservative privileged groups? Candidates and political leaders who were perceived to be a real threat to the status quo, such as Reverend Martin Luther King Jr., Malcolm X, and Robert F. Kennedy, were unfortunately assassinated. Conservative and "liberal" privileged Whites who now claim they stand behind Obama because they believe in what he represents, decided to become part of a political and historical phenomenon when they realized they could not stop it: the Obama phenomenon. They might have allowed Obama to run the show while influencing the political and socioeconomic apparatus to satisfy their own interests. Or, to put it bluntly, they might have used Obama to put on a political show giving people of color and poor Whites the illusion that they are at last entering a participatory democratic era after decades of hegemonic domination of the US political and economic systems by conservative and privileged Whites.

Should one trust Obama's political decisions? The majority of his appointees are the same conservative political figures such as Secretary of Education Arne Duncan, former Secretary of Defense Robert Gates, retired General James Jones, and former Secretary of Treasury Larry Summers, who all have maintained and profited from the US voucher capitalist system for decades. Obama's secretary of education, Arne Duncan, who was the CEO of the Chicago Public Schools, has a long-standing record of corporatizing and militarizing the third largest school system in the nation, a public school system that is approximately 90 percent poor minority students (Giroux & Saltman, 2008). Giroux and Saltman (2008) state that, "Under Duncan, Chicago took the lead in creating public schools run as military academies, vastly expanded draconian student expulsions, instituted sweeping surveillance practices, advocated a growing police presence in the schools, arbitrarily shut down entire schools and fired entire school staffs" (p. 2).

What could educators and parents have expected of a secretary of education with such a record? And what should have they expected of President Obama, who appointed him? Obama did not seem to have the courage to move from his rhetoric of hope, change, and unity, to make substantive educational, socioeconomic, and political decisions that would improve the dire conditions of poor people of color and Whites. Even though people involved in grassroots movement and progressive social and political organizations mobilized and organized so they could make Obama's slogan "Change From the Bottom Up" become a reality, Obama did virtually nothing to keep his grand promise.

As Obama is ending his second term, it does not appear that that he would take concrete executive decisions to protect the environment, to provide quality education, to challenge US imperialism and capitalism, and to create greater socioeconomic opportunities for everyone, as he might have seemed to promise during his two presidential campaigns. With continuous political pressure from people involved in these movements and organizations, it was hoped that fundamental changes would occur during Obama's term, but such changes did not happen. The unanswered questions remain: What kind of President Barack Obama will be remembered? One who created space in his administration for the voice of progressive educators and intellectuals, social activists, ordinary and concerned citizens to be heard before making decisions that educationally, economically, and politically would impact their lives? Or a president who, before making crucial political decisions like sending more troops to Afghanistan and Iraq to kill innocent people and get killed, only listened to conservative and privileged White males in his cabinet who have maintained and greatly profited from this voucher capitalist and racist system for decades? His foreign policy, which expanded the war in Afghanistan, have been responsible for the killing of innocent people abroad, including US citizens, through drone strikes. This suggests that Obama has aligned himself with the oligarchic groups who are pro-imperialist and have controlled the economy and the political apparatus of this country for decades. As West states, "He's [Barack Obama] ended up being the black mascot of the Wall Street oligarchs and corporate plutocrats!" (West, as cited in Thompson, 2011, p. 1).

Conclusion

Seven years into his presidency, Obama has shown little willingness to make political and economic decisions that would benefit the poor and the struggling middle class to whom he has constantly referred in his political speech. Given his political record—including his draconian decision to deport more undocumented immigrants than his White male predecessors; his authorization to kill citizens, including American citizens, through drone strikes; and his government spying on citizens—there is no reason to believe that Obama would implement policies that would ameliorate the miserable socioeconomic conditions of those in need as he completes his term as president in a year. Nor should one be so foolish as to believe his legacy would contribute to improve race relations in this country. As Steinberg (2011) notes, "I believe Obama's presidency does nothing for racial relations in the US, except possibly allow more racist behavior to tacitly come forward in blocking appropriate legislation" (p. 65). Obama has been used and will continue to be used beyond his presidency as a proxy to cover up the continuous savage working and living conditions of people of color and poor Whites. He is given to us as a Black trophy president to camouflage the continued harmful effects of White supremacy and voucher capitalism on the lives of the oppressed, particularly poor people of color and poor Whites.

3
OBAMA: TRAPPED AT THE CROSSROAD OF BLACK MASCULINITY AND WHITE PATRIARCHY

If the white man challenges my humanity, I will impose my whole weight as a man on his life and show him that I am not that "sho' good eatin'" that he persists in imagining. I find myself suddenly in the world and I recognize that I have one right alone: That of demanding human behavior from the other. One duty alone: That of not renouncing my freedom through my choices. I have no wish to be the victim of the Fraud of a black world. My life should not be devoted to drawing up the balance sheet of Negro values. There is no white world, there is no white ethic, anymore than there is a white intelligence. There are in every part of the world men who search. I am not a prisoner of history. I should not seek there for the meaning of my destiny.

(Fanon, 1967, p. 228)

What interests me about Obama's rise is the tension that intellectuals cannot seem to resolve. We hear two types of arguments. One, Obama's inauguration surely signals the end of U.S. racism as we know it. If a Black person can become president, then racial disparities are explainable through differences in effort and random chance and not through structural racism. This rationalization has rightly been called color blindness and an excess of racial optimism. Two, and opposing this view, to some intellectuals Obama's victory represents the latest (not the last) chapter in White supremacy because it is predicted that Obama will neither radically change the racial landscape nor advocates for race-based initiatives. The upshot is that a Black man for president becomes another alibi for White tolerance, and we should be suspicious of White interests that converge with the Black plight. This sentiment may rightly fall under racial realism, even pessimism.

(Leonardo, 2011, p. 40)

Introduction

Drawing on data from a previous study conducted on Black masculinity and racism (Orelus, 2010), this chapter analyzes how the White mainstream corporate media have misrepresented Black masculinity. Further, this chapter examines the manner in which poor Blacks, particularly poor Black males, have been perceived and poorly treated in society. In addition, this chapter examines ways and the degree to which religious beliefs and cultural norms have influenced the way many men of African descent perceive women's role in society. Finally, it examines the implications of ideological mechanism that privileged White males have put in place to promote tokenized men and women of color, like President Barack Obama, while demonizing those who dare challenge White supremacy and patriarchy.

Black Masculinity and White Patriarchy

From slavery until now, men of African descent have been ideologically conditioned to emulate the form of masculinity that Western White supremacist and capitalist men have legislated, enacted, and imposed on them and on other men (Orelus, 2010). Black and Brown men who have refused to mimic and reproduce this form of masculinity are often seen and treated as the "other." Many of them have been harshly criticized for being Afro-centric, that is, for embracing and talking about their African cultural roots with pride (Asante, 2011). Furthermore, Black and Brown men who have chosen not to speak, behave, and act like White Western men are often portrayed as less intelligent. However, those who have appropriated and mastered the White male dominant discourse, like Obama, have been called articulate, clean, and smart Black men by individual Whites, particularly by hegemonic White males.

Former US Senator Joe Biden, President Barack Obama's vice president, placed a "clean, smart, and articulate Black man" label on Barack Obama during the presidential campaign. Vice President Biden, then a senator, stated, "I mean, you got the first mainstream African-American who is articulate and bright and clean and a nice-looking guy. I mean, that's a storybook, man" (Biden, as cited in Tapper, 2007). Senator Joe Biden was criticized for his comment, taken as offensive to the intelligence of many prominent African American and Black intellectuals such as Cornel West.

However, ironically about a year later, he was chosen as Obama's running mate. This choice once more confirms that whiteness is a privilege that enables many dominant White males to get away with hurtful comments they make about other ethnic and racial groups. This choice also confirms that White men control the political power of this country. They can use their White male privilege to either demonize people of color, especially those who dare challenge White supremacy and the status quo, or "promote" a few of them as "good citizens" who embrace their ideology and therefore do not constitute a threat to their interests. This applies to a great extent to Obama whom, during his presidential campaign and particularly during the convention of the Democratic Party in 2008, many privileged White men and women represented as a different kind of Black man. They represented him as one of their kind. Trying to show similarity between himself and Obama, Senator Joe Biden stated in his acceptance speech for the vice president in 2008, "Barack Obama and I took very different journeys to this destination, but we share a common destiny" (Biden, as cited in Orelus, 2010, p. 124).

Although Obama's blackness is physically visible, symbolically Obama was represented merely as an American at the Democratic convention. He was not constantly referred to as a Black man as throughout the presidential campaign before his nomination. Unlike his rival Hillary Clinton, who was called a strong female candidate, Obama was called a Black, an African American candidate. While his blackness and race were placed at the forefront of the political debate, Hillary's whiteness and race were not. Furthermore—unlike his White male rivals who were never called White candidates but merely candidates—Obama was always the Black, the African American candidate. However, this discourse of racial representation of Obama as a candidate suddenly disappeared during the convention of the Democratic Party. Through all the speeches that many privileged White men and women made to support Obama, they called him a good American, a good citizen who loves his country and who can bring people together. James, a 38-year-old participant in a previous study that I conducted (Orelus, 2010), captured the way the mainstream media controlled by rich White males represented Obama while he was running for president:

> He's a hybrid individual; he comes from both traditions. Right now, he is the most newsworthy black man in the world. He may be not the most important black man right now, but he is the one at the center of the news most frequently in contemporary times, and if he becomes president, that will continue. Because Barack Obama is hybrid, meaning he comes from both worlds, he's been embraced by many Americans and many members of the elite establishment as a negotiator. That is, someone who can negotiate and bridge these two worlds, black and white. What allows him to potentially become a stabilizing force in a world, which is still restrictive after 40 years of postcolonial era, is his hybrid nature. People are looking toward the future. He has this unique international appeal for being someone who can help to stabilize the relationship between People of African descent, White, Asians, and others. For that same reason, he is also embraced in America to help stabilize the relationship between the dominant and colonized people, African Americans and other people of African descents (James, as cited in Orelus, 2010, p. 124).

In many respects, the mainstream media represented and continues to represent Obama as someone who symbolizes the American dream. Many conservative White males through their political rhetoric claimed they and Obama shared this dream. What about other prominent Black or African American leaders? They do not represent the American dream that "we" all share because they are not "clean and articulate" like Obama, as Vice President Joe Biden's comment suggests? Biden's comment about Obama is not anything new. It goes as far back as the slavery period. During slavery, the slaves who were assimilated in the White mainstream discourse and emulated the White male masters were seen as less threatening; they were used as tokens. These tokenized slaves received slightly better treatment than those who chose to resist White supremacy and refused to emulate the White male discourse and way of life. In postslavery era, White supremacists and capitalists have used Black tokens to maintain the status quo. They have uplifted the few Black and Brown men whom they feel speak and behave like them while denigrating and isolating those who refuse to embrace the mainstream discourse and go along with the rules of the White male racist games. West (1993) maintains, "Only certain kinds of Black people deserve high positions, that is, those who accept the rules of the game played by White America" (p. 42).

Black Male Tokenism and Racial Division: Privileged Whites' Tactics to Maintain the Status Quo

No one can deny that racism exists whether one claims that it is a human invention, it is socially constructed, or it is biologically determined. The question, then, becomes: How has the White conservative dominant class used racism to exploit and oppress people of color? To the same degree as sexism and imperialism, racism is an abstract concept. However, its victims can easily feel its negative effects. One can spend centuries debating about the origin of racism, but it is unquestionable that it is an oppressive tool that has been institutionalized and used to reduce Black/Brown people and other subordinate groups to the economic, social, and political margins. Whether subtle or overt, this tool is still functional and constitutes an obstacle to windows of opportunities to people of color. Strategically, along with this tool the White conservative dominant class has used a few Black tokens at various institutions to avoid racial turmoil and/or massive Black revolt (like the slaves' revolt in Santo Domingo that led to the independence of Haiti in 1804).

Black tokenism is a White male supremacist strategy that has been used to put a veil on the racist structure of the US society. Further, it is a subtle form of racism that might be as oppressive and dangerous as other forms of racism that people of color have experienced. For example, if one is dealing with a "naked form of racism," as has been the case in the United States, particularly during the Jim Crow era, and in South Africa for decades, one will know what strategies to use in order to protect oneself from being lynched in the street by the Ku Klux

Klan. However, when people of color are faced with a form of racism that is not quite as visible as it was before, they simply become more vulnerable than ever.

For instance, one might naïvely believe that the few Black and Brown people who are appointed to a high governmental position, or hired as managers or assistant managers at huge corporations/institutions would protect people of color from racial injustice. However, what one fails to understand is that these Black and Brown employees or appointees are often used by the system to falsify or cover up the tragic economic and social realities of people of color. In fact, once they are in these conditioned positions these modern "house Negroes" often try not to identify with people of color who live in housing projects and slums. They are assigned a very specific mission, which consists of maintaining the White status quo at the expense of their Black and Brown brothers and sisters' misery and inhuman conditions.

These modern house Negroes usually do not serve the interest of other people of color but their own and that of the White dominant class. Whether they embrace the Republican or the Democratic doctrines, the fact remains that these Black or Brown puppets are brainwashed by the White supremacy racist ideology to participate in the perpetuation of a racist system that is hostile and oppressive to people of color. Malcolm X intelligently captured this dirty game that the White dominant class has been playing against Black people since slavery.

Modern house Negroes can be found at multiple levels of the racist economic and social pyramid. They can be found, for example, in schools, social agencies, hospitals, and in the hotel industry. This handful of house Negroes are usually hired or appointed by these institutions to promote so-called racial diversity. However, once indoctrinated by the White supremacist ideology of the system, they sometimes turn out to be as hostile and oppressive to people of color as some White racist individuals. For example, one might walk into or work at a place that is run by a person of color and naïvely think that he or she will be at least protected from institutionalized racial discrimination. This, in my view, is simply an illusion, for a White supremacist system will remain a racist system no matter who is running it—unless people organize collectively to radically change it.

I am reminded of a discussion about institutionalized racism that I had with several of my liberal White colleagues and friends whose partners were Black. Through this discussion I soon realized that most of them struggled to admit the fact that their White skin color puts them in a far better position than their Black partners. As their defensive mechanism, they referred to President Barack Obama and a few people of color, such as the two former African American former secretaries of state, Colin Powell and Condoleezza Rice who obviously held key governmental positions. To substantiate their argument, they also referred to the Protestant ethic conceived by the French sociologist Émile Durkheim. According to this sociological and philosophical view, anyone can be successful if they work very hard. What my White colleagues failed to understand was that, as Cornel West (1993) states, "It is the innumerable cases in which black people do act on the Protestant ethic and still remain at the bottom of the social ladder. Instead, they highlight the few instances in which blacks ascend to the top, as if such success is available to all blacks, regardless of circumstances" (p. 34).

When the discussion got heated, some of my liberal White colleagues and classmates conceded, confessing that they feel ashamed of all the ugly things that some White people have done to people of color. For instance, one who claimed to be a White ally got angry and exploded, shouting, "I hate my people! It is unconceivable that White people have done all these terrible things to people of color; I wonder if they have a human heart." Obviously, my colleagues missed the point that I was trying to make. I was trying to make them realize that having a few token Blacks here and there at some institutions does not necessarily transform the White supremacist system. They failed to grasp the point that I was trying to make, and they shifted the focus of the discussion from institutionalized racism to individual racism.

Returning to Black male tokenism, I wish to narrate a painful experience that my coworkers of color and I had with an African American manager working at one of the most prestigious hotels in Boston, Massachusetts. This male manager had started working at this place as an overnight housekeeper and was, unlike his female Black coworkers, quickly promoted to a managerial position. Despite all the racist exploitation and injustice that employees of color faced at that place, he did not stop lying about, betraying his male coworkers, and crawling until he became the manager of a less-desirable department within the hotel, valet parking.

Although his behavior and personality disgusted us while he was a housekeeper, we were all happy to have him as the first Black manager at the hotel. Nevertheless, it did not take us long to realize that he was just a Black puppet being put in a managerial position to serve the capitalist interest of the company. Within three months, he was used as a facade in all activities and advertising videos of the hotel. Unlike White male managers at other departments, they made him work long hours while his salary was a lot less than any of these White managers. Yet, this house Negro did not stop bragging about his new position and making his Black employees work a lot harder than anybody else to protect his job.

I witnessed the privilege that some of my White male coworkers enjoyed. They were able to get flexible hours and went on vacation whenever they wanted; they showed up late to work quite often, but did not get punished. However, the Black and Latino workers who were forced to work long hours and expected to work extremely hard could take a vacation only when it would not jeopardize the Black manager's position and the hotel CEO's corporate interests. In other words, they were allowed to take some time off only when they were not needed to give their blood to maximize the hotel's profits. This horrible experience has strengthened my conviction that house Negroes have by and large contributed to maintain racism and deepen the sharp economic gap that exists between the poor Black and White and the capitalist class.

All in all, modern house Negroes can be as dangerous as some racist White people. They may represent a threat and/or an obstacle to the Black movement liberation, because they can be easily manipulated and used by this patriarchal, capitalist, and White supremacist system to make racism less visible than before. The false promise and/or the order that many of them often seem to receive from their modern "White masters" is the following: Do what you are told; forget about where you come from. More importantly, do not question White male supremacy, and we will give the illusion that you can get close to the top of the economic and political pyramid.

In the case of President Barack Obama, for example, his ability to code switch between the White dominant discourse and the African vernacular discourse looks appealing to both liberal and conservative White groups. This, therefore, enabled him to create a place for himself among conservative and privileged White males. Of course, this did not happen in a void. As noted in the first chapter, being raised by a White family and having the opportunity to attend an elitist university, Harvard University, where he earned a law degree, enabled him to acquire the White dominant discourse. James goes on to point out:

> For a long time, it was only musicians, and then it was only athletes. Currently, we have a politician. This particular politician was raised by his grandparents on his mother side. He went to elite American institutions such as Harvard, which has been a training ground for the ruling elites and the leadership of the entire colonial establishment. I'd say that this colonial establishment is completely a part of the larger dominant establishment (James, as cited in Orelus, 2010, p. 129).

Obama's long apprenticeship in the White dominant male discourse might explain why his stance and discourse on race issues have been different from those of many African American leaders and prominent Black intellectuals, like Jesse Jackson, Eduardo Bonilla-Silva, and Cornel West, among others. In fact, Obama avoided talking about race during his campaign, as he knew doing so would jeopardize his victory. As Bonilla-Silva eloquently pointed out:

> He [Obama] avoided using the term *racism* in his campaign. Actually the only time that he used it was to chastise Reverend Wright who claimed that racism was endemic. However, according to Obama, it [racism] has not been endemic in America, which suggests that Reverend Wright is crazy. He has obviously made a color-blind appeal, a nationalistic appeal by saying so. Obama is famous for saying, "I don't see a black America, I don't see a white America, I only see the United States of America." He needs to go to an eye doctor and get some new glasses so he can see the white America, the black America and the Latino America, etc. (Bonilla-Silva, 2011, p. 129).

Had Obama not been forced to deliver a speech on race after his former pastor and close friend Reverend Jeremiah Wright made some controversial statements about US imperialism and legal system, perhaps he would have continued to remain silent about the race issue. Reverend Wright stated, "Barack knows what it means to be a Black man living in a country and a culture that is controlled by rich, White people. Hillary ain't never been called a n——." While sharing his view about this controversy, Joe, another participant in the same study (Orelus, 2010), said:

> I think what's going on between Obama and Reverend Wright, the way the media has been using that . . . the way in which blacks have been buying . . . the way the media interprets this situation is wrong, problematic. It's very problematic—the conditions that Black men are in right now. I think that Reverend Wright and Obama are just equally good Black people, but the world wants us to see Obama as good and Wright as bad, and too many people immediately would buy into that. And that's very problematic, in my view (Joe, as cited in Orelus, 2010, p. 132).

The controversy that occurred as a result of Reverend Wright's comments is significant in that it can help us unveil what form of discourse is privileged over others in the White mainstream media. All forms of discourse are political and ideological. If a discourse reflects the dominant ideology, it often tends to be normalized and becomes part of the public consciousness. For example, for those who have striven to build and maintain US imperialism and the White patriarchal system from which they have greatly benefited, Reverend Wright's comments would be a threat to their interests. These privileged people's main goal is to keep the nation in a dormant, silenced state so their corporate interests will not be challenged. However, for many Black/Brown people who have been victimized by US imperialism and its unfair legal, economic, educational, and political systems and foreign policy, they might not have interpreted Reverend Wright's as inflammatory and divisive. In fact, for marginalized, occupied, and neocolonized people, Wright's comments might only confirm what they have always thought about this country in terms of the way it has treated marginalized people here and abroad.

Reverend Wright was not the first reverend who publicly made controversial comments. Nor was Obama the first political figure associated with a mentor-pastor who was not afraid of expressing his political views publicly. The important question that one should ask oneself then is: Who has been allowed by this White patriarchal system to make controversial statements without being harshly criticized and jeopardizing the political career of his or her friends and male leaders? There are many in the United States and elsewhere in the world. But let us take the prime example of the well-known White American, Reverend Pat Robertson.

Reverend Robertson is notorious for making racist, sexist, homophobic, and xenophobic comments about marginalized groups in society; yet, none of the political leaders whom he endorsed was asked to distance themselves from him. Furthermore, none of the White male leaders Reverend Robertson supported became the main target of the mainstream media and suffered political loss for associating themselves with him. As an example, during the 2008 presidential campaign, Reverend Robertson endorsed the Republican candidate Rudy Giuliani. The media did not go after Giuliani like they pressed Obama to distance himself from Reverend Wright. As Jeff Stanglin (2008) observed: "Pat Robertson, the same pastor who said what Nazi Germany did to the Jews is the same thing that liberals and homosexuals are doing to America, regularly endorses Republican candidates" (p. 1) Stanglin went on to point out:

> John Hagee, the ardent pro-Israel leader of the 19,000-member Cornerstone Church in San Antonio, endorsed John McCain in late February. Outside his own church, Hagee is best known for calling the Catholic Church "The Great Whore" and for blaming New Orleans residents and their sins for Hurricane Katrina. Despite these and other divisive comments, however, McCain has accepted Hagee's endorsement. Whether McCain actually stands behind the comments or whether he is simply pandering to the religious right is up for speculation. For America's sake, it needs to be the latter (2008, p. 2).

Along the same lines, Bill Berkowitz (2006) stated:

> While the Reverend Pat Robertson was flayed recently over his suggestion that Israeli Prime Minister Ariel Sharon's stroke was an act of retribution by God for the transfer of land in the Gaza Strip to the Palestinians, the Reverend's charitable organization, Operation Blessing, was raking in wads of faith-based money from the Bush Administration (p. 1).

What all this suggests is that any powerful White man who is the pillar of the White supremacist and patriarchal system can make comments that are hurtful to oppressed groups and still go unpunished. The way the media have treated Reverend Wright, as opposed to the way Reverend Robertson has been treated, confirms that whiteness and social class matter. It is true that both reverends Jeremiah Wright and Pat Robertson are two privileged males. However, due to their different racial identity and background, Pat Robinson is ranked at a more hegemonic male position in the US society than is Jeremiah Wright.

This explains why Reverend Robertson has been able to abuse his hegemonic male position without being harshly criticized by the mass corporate media. Instead of criticizing and punishing him for all the sexist, racist, homophobic, and xenophobic statements he has been making, CEOs of corporate media have allowed him to be on the air with his Sunday show. Through this show, he continues to offend people who have been placed at the margins due to their poor social class, racial, sexual orientation, linguistic, and cultural backgrounds.

Obviously, Reverend Robertson is a well-known White male figure who has been at the fore of heated debates about controversial issues like homosexuality, racism, and the like. There are other privileged or nonprivileged White men and women who have made racist and homophobic statements in other contexts, but the media have shied away from them. Similarly, there may be many Black men and women of color who share Reverend Jeremiah Wright's views. However, because of their social class, they are not in a hegemonic male position to express their views in a way that would enable them to reach a larger audience other than their friends, family, and colleagues. Social class and race matter; they determine which category of men are allowed to speak on behalf of whom. Both Jeremiah Wright and Pat Robertson symbolize these types of men by virtue of their social class and position in society, although the latter has been placed in far more hegemonic position than the former because of his whiteness. Nonetheless, irrespective of their social class and race, men are given more opportunities to be heard than women are. However, a clear distinction ought to be made between privileged men, especially privileged White men, who have been allowed more space by the patriarchal and racist system to talk with authority, and marginalized men and women who are often expected to listen and remain silent.

Obama, Black Masculinity, Social Class, and Sexual Orientation

As expected, privileged, heterosexual Black and Brown men often have performed their relatively dominant masculinity differently than poor and marginalized straight, bisexual, transgender, and gay Black/Brown men. Many of these privileged, straight Black and Brown men, among others, have tried to emulate the model of masculinity that privileged and straight White men have sold to the world through the mass media and canonical texts. They often try to associate themselves with the social, political, and ideological club to which privileged, straight White men belong. Moreover, they often share the conservative ideology that these privileged, straight White men hold. In addition, many of these Brown and Black men are convinced that the best and fastest way to move up socially, economically, and politically is to find ways to enter the White world. Finally, by embracing the White culture and ideology, they sometimes become the prey of privileged White males, who use them politically to generalize about the so-called social mobility of Black people.

Instead of furthering the political and economic struggles of people of African descent, the masculinity of privileged Blacks has been an ideological veil masking the miserable conditions of poor Black men and women. Privileged White males and females often perceive this category of men of African descent as "good Black and Brown men," for they pose no threat to their hegemonic interests. These very few good and educated Black and Brown men usually graduate from elite schools such as Harvard University, which mold and apprentice them into the White dominant discourse and ideology.

Whether they attend these elite schools because they are from a privileged background or they are poor but work hard academically, these "good and educated Black men" sometimes graduate with an agenda to move up economically, socially, and politically at any cost. They often acquire the elitist, mercantilist, and capitalist way of conceiving the world: that is, the educated and the powerful have to dominate and conquer the world. Dominating and conquering the world is usually, if not always, done at the expense of poor and marginalized people of color.

However, this acquired or learned White male elitist mentality of dominating and conquering the world does not apply to all men of African descent who have graduated from Ivy League school. Historically, Ivy League–educated Black and Brown men such as W.E.B. Dubois, Randall Robinson, and Cornel West have chosen to embrace the struggles of ordinary Black people. Many educated men of African descent often aspire to become rich and live a bourgeois life style. After earning their degrees, they usually do not return to the marginalized neighborhoods where they grew up. They seek to live in affluent White and/or Black neighborhoods. This does not happen in a vacuum.

Many of these men of African descent learn through school and from family members and the media that they must be highly educated and economically powerful in order to be able to compete with and be accepted by the White world. That they have to leave behind their past, including the neighborhood where they received their basic education and where their close and distant family members still live, in order to feel they are achieving and living the American dream. Unfortunately, many privileged and educated men of African descent have embraced this ideology. These men ideologically and symbolically cross the racial line so they can be "welcomed" and "embraced" by the elite, White world.

President Obama, along with US Supreme Court Justice Clarence Thomas and General Colin Powell, among others, fall into this category of Black men whose skin tone might be dark and brown but their ideology is White. Privileged Black men like them do not perform their masculinity the same way as ordinary Black men do. Their social and political performance of masculinity is different. This is intrinsically linked to factors such as social class and power.

Power, in this context, is not defined the way Foucault (1980) defined it. In other words, it is not something that is fluid, circulated through our bodies, and places itself into our attitudes, daily actions, and discourses, and to which everyone has access. Instead, the form of power to which I am alluding here is linked to privileged Black and Brown men's hegemonic, social, political, intellectual, and economic capital (Bourdieu, 1990). President Barack Obama is an example of how these different forms of capital can transcend, albeit superficially, the biological characteristics and historical aspects of Black masculinity.

Unlike many African Americans and other Blacks in this country, Barack Obama earned a law degree from Harvard University, worked as a community organizer and as a civil rights attorney, was elected to the US Senate, and ran for president to become the Obama the whole world now knows. Furthermore, the mainstream media has represented Obama as a Black man who grew up with a liberated and privileged mindset. Moreover, given the political, ideological, and social club to which President Obama currently belongs, it would be inaccurate to compare his masculinity to that of a poor, gay, biracial Black man. Privileged, straight, and Christian White men dominating this club have controlled the wealth of this country for centuries. Therefore, by association, Obama's masculinity symbolically and ideologically reflects the hegemonic interests of these straight, privileged White men who have legislated and enacted the patriarchal rules.

Some of participants taking part in the study referred to earlier (Orelus, 2010) capture what I articulated about Obama's, Clarence Thomas' and Colin Powell's social class, which differentiates them from many ordinary Black men, especially from gay Black and Brown men. For example, in my interview with Tom and Dr. Joe, it was clear that they understand the difference between these privileged Black and Brown men's masculinity and that of poor working men. Linking Obama's masculinity to his social class and political status and comparing him to ordinary men of African descent, Tom stated:

> People define Obama only as a black man, not understanding that his class has a lot to do with the way he performs as a man. The fact that he is a graduate of Harvard, that he is a lawyer, that he is in the senate, that he is in one of the most exclusive

clubs in the country, in the world I would say, these things are specifically related to his class which allows him to connect with other white rich men who see him as maybe a hopeful alternative to the Bush legacy. But they are also connecting with his maleness. This is where blackness becomes a little less . . . it's not the sole definer of Obama. I don't want to get into ferocity of . . . if he was a black man he wouldn't be where he is. But I think it's also because the fact that he is already in the senate; he's the only black person in the senate, which illustrates he already has a certain amount of privilege. So I think it's important to recognize that because in society most people see him only as a black person. But I think there are certain elites that see him as many more things and are able to connect on those different levels. But if you take his sense of blackness and you compare it to ours, but I think we even have some privileged being college education and PhDs. But if you take someone who is working class, driving a bus day in and day out, there is definitely very little that connects them. They may be both men; they may both be quarter black, but their class is going to divide them because the fact is that Obama is making a million dollars a year, writing books and all these things, and this man is probably making $40,000 a year driving a bus (Tom, as cited in Orelus, 2010, p. 154).

What can be inferred from the analysis of Obama's case is that Black masculinity and maleness is not biologically static: it is fluid and can take different ideological and political forms depending on the context, the circumstances, and one's hegemonic interests. In other words, different forms of Black masculinities can be performed ideologically, politically, and socially to reach certain goals. Obama, unquestionably, has found ways to transcend his blackness to perform a form of masculinity that fits the logic of the White supremacist and patriarchal system. As Dr. Joe bluntly put it, "Unless you're Obama or maybe Clarence Thomas who are kissing a lot of White butt, you're not gonna get into the White boys clubs" (Dr. Joe, as cited in Orelus, 2010, p. 45).

It is worth emphasizing that President Barack Obama, General Colin Powell, and Supreme Court Justice Thomas are isolated cases and therefore do not reflect the daily reality of men of African descent, particularly queer Black men. As Tom went on to say:

A gay black man is quadruply oppressed because of his race, his color, his class, and sexual orientation. I think that in the black community often times it's even more harsh for black gay man. That also demonstrates that there is . . . you can't look at masculinity as sort of a linear thing; it is very complicated, and each of this social location kind of come in and makes people's lives different. So I think Obama is a good example, but you take a gay black man, it's a totally different experience, maybe even more difficult because he is fighting against the oppression of the same black communities, like saying he is not one of us. So it's a complicated issue (Tom, as cited in Orelus, 2010, p. 56).

Conclusion

President Obama's performance of masculinity as a straight, Christian, highly educated, and privileged Black male is in stark contrast with the public performance of poor Blacks and marginalized groups, such as queer males of color. Furthermore, his political victory has not and will not erase the fact that men of African descent have been portrayed as violent, rapists, lazy, and drug dealers. For this reason and others, it is naïve to think that Obama's presidency would lead to fundamental, structural change in the US political system. Going beyond Obama's presidency, we ought to critically examine ways and the degree to which the legacy of slavery and colonialism and factors such as social class and sexual orientation have impacted the masculinity of men of color. Last, we ought to unpack the manner in which hegemonic groups have portrayed and circulated through the mainstream media an oppressive, violent, and aggressive form of Black masculinity, which is often feared. This misrepresentation of Black masculinity needs to be challenged and uprooted for racial and gender justice and liberation.

4

OBAMA VS. POSTCOLONIAL AFRICAN LEADERS
Who Is the New Oppressor?

I have been a long-standing supporter of Obama, and I also worked in his campaign. I have seen many of his positions in terms of governing as opposed to campaigning, necessary pragmatic alternatives to the purer arguments he offers in his books and speeches. Although of course he must be pragmatic, he is far too cautious, often reluctant to lead. He often abandons essential ideas and positions far too easily, in my view. His caution, if not timidity, on the economy has led to lost opportunities. That was an instance where he abandoned anti-corporate popular sentiment—there's some class consciousness for you, to the authoritarian populist right wing. That was a big mistake. His war in Afghanistan is another big mistake.

(Howard Winant, 2011, p. 62)

Introduction

The long-term psychological effects of colonization on "postcolonial subjects" are deeper than one can imagine. Even though European colonizers are no longer established in the colony, the colonial seed they planted in and left behind continues to sprout. This seed has continued to grow in the minds and consciousness of many people, including those who have occupied key political positions in former colonized lands, like Mozambique, Burkina Faso, the Congo, and the United States, after the colonial era ended. In these lands, many emerging political leaders often show signs of internalized racism expressed through their behavior and actions. For example, political leaders in formerly colonized or occupied lands have reproduced abusive practices similar to those of former European colonizers. These practices have been occurring in the United States as well. Specifically, like postcolonial African leaders and presidents, American presidents emerging after colonization have historically displaced and removed indigenous people from their lands, and they have displayed oppressive behaviors and actions such as spying on citizens, sending police officers to repress dissident voices, and implementing oppressive policies affecting people's lives. These practices are similar to those of former European colonizers, namely the British, who during colonization seized the land of indigenous people, utilized some colonized people to spy on others, and used oppressive measures to repress those who rebelled against the status quo—all for the maintenance of the colonial rules. This chapter sheds light on these issues by analyzing the political actions of some African leaders, particularly Joseph Mugabe, and Barack Obama, the first American man of color to be elected president since the United States gained its independence from the British colonial power.

As historically documented, postcolonial African leaders, like Blaise Compaoré and Mobuto Sese Seko, were supported by Western governments to overthrow and kill progressive leaders like Thomas Sankara and the late Congolese prime minister, Patrice Lumumba, respectively (Gerard & Kuklick, 2015; Harsh, 2014). Mobuto murdered Lumumba with the support and complicity of the Belgian and US governments (Gerard & Kuklick, 2015; Zeilig, 2008). These two governments portrayed Lumumba as a prime minister who was contaminating the whole continent of Africa with his socialist agenda; they financed and helped orchestrate his assassination (De Witte, 2002; Gerard & Kuklick, 2015). Lumumba's well-planned and executed murder was not an isolated case.

Allen Dulles, then head of the Central Intelligence Agency (CIA), stated that "Lumumba's removal must be an urgent and prime objective" of covert action, not least because US investments might have been endangered by what internal documents refer to as "radical nationalists" (Dulles, as cited in Chomsky, 2014, p. 1). Along the same lines, Chomsky (2014) observes, "Under the supervision of Belgian officers,

Lumumba was murdered, realizing President Eisenhower's wish that he 'would fall into a river full of crocodiles.' Congo was handed over to the U.S. favorite, the murderous and corrupt dictator Mobutu Sese Seko, and on to today's wreckage of Africa's hopes" (p. 2).

The former leader of Burkina Faso, Thomas Sankara, is also a prime example. Sankara was assassinated by Blaise Compaoré, whom the French and US governments supported in his coup d'état leading to the overthrow of Sankara. Like Patrice Lumumba, Thomas Sankara was an anti-imperialist and anticolonialist leader who fearlessly spoke against Western exploitation of Africa. Both were champions of the poor and the colonized. Because of their ideological and political positions, they were assassinated. Historically, imperialist Western powers such as the United States, Great Britain, and France have shown much dedication to and used all kinds of imperialist strategies to topple governments that pose a threat to their geopolitical and economic interests.

As long as the corporate interests of these Western countries are maintained and protected, it does not matter if the puppet governments they help put in power are abusing people's inalienable human rights. Nor does it matter if genocide occurs among various ethnic groups as a result of their invasion and occupation, so long as their interests are not in danger (Chomsky, 2004). For example, these powerful Western countries witnessed the genocide occurring in Rwanda, yet did nothing to stop it. Even though they were selling deadly weapons to antagonist military or civilian armed groups to kill one another, they showed no concern for those who were massacred, including pregnant women, children, and the elderly. These colonial and imperialist countries created a chaotic situation in their former colonies, leading to division among different ethnic and religious groups from varying social class and linguistic backgrounds.

The divisive colonial seeds planted in colonized lands have continued to propagate even decades after the colonizers left. Specifically, the oppressive practices that the colonizer used to subjugate colonized Africans have been redesigned and reproduced by many authoritarian African leaders, like former Congolese president Mobutu Sese Seko, Joseph Mugabe in Zimbabwe, and former president of Burkina Faso, Blaise Compaoré, among others. These African leaders, who took over political power relatively soon after their countries gained their independence, have used oppressive measures, such as cracking down on dissident voices, to remain in power. In some cases, they have murdered political opponents while maintaining the masses in abject poverty and dark ignorance.

Close colleagues and students from Zimbabwe have shared with me that it is uncommon, for example, to find Zimbabwean citizens able to publically criticize Mugabe without fearing for their safety. The irony is that like ordinary African civilians, "postcolonial" African political leaders suffered enormously during the colonial terror established and normalized in their native land. Further, even though many were highly educated (some of them were educated in the West), they still suffered social humiliation and racial discrimination from the colonial regime. It did not matter if they were people with PhDs; they were treated as the "wretched of the earth" (Fanon, 1963) in their own land. In other words, regardless of their class privileges, Africans suffered during colonial domination and occupation of their land.

The level of suffering, of course, varied across social class as well as other factors such as skin color, for colorism mattered a great deal during the colonial period. Those who were light skinned and went along with the status quo were better off than the dark-skinned poor. Despite the fact that for decades now colonialism has been officially demolished and eliminated (at least in theory) in African countries, the debate about light skin vs. dark skin continues to occur in these countries today. Because of the colonial legacy, light-skinned people are perceived to be and seen as less threatening to the White power structure than those with dark skin. Consequently, they have been given more opportunities than dark-skinned people of color to navigate through the White supremacist system for professional advancement (Orelus, 2013).

With respect to political leaders emerging after the colonial era, many have become nearly as oppressive as their former colonizers or slave masters. Like the former colonizer or slave master, they dehumanize, objectify, brutalize, murder, or assassinate dissidents. For example, before Mugabe came to power, he was seen as a progressive leader concerned for the well-being of oppressed Zimbabweans.

As both prime minister and president, he has put in place social and educational programs aimed at helping marginalized Zimbabweans. However, to stay in power, Mugabe has become increasingly oppressive (Meredith, 2007)—although he might not be as oppressive as the Western media have portrayed him to be. Mugabe represents a threat to the geopolitical and economic interests of the United States and the UK. Consequently, these two countries have portrayed a very negative image of Mugabe, whose political decisions and actions have become increasingly independent of the West. History has shown that Western powers, like the United States, the UK, and France do not like leaders who are too independent, and Mugabe fits this description.

Mugabe deserves much credit for his courage to challenge Western imperialism. He also deserves recognition for trying, especially during the early years of his presidency, to institute land reform, which probably would have led to an equal and equitable distribution of land among Zimbabweans had it been successfully implemented. Finally, his nationalist fervor and his socialist idealism for an equitable, strong, and economically and politically independent Zimbabwe must be acknowledged. However, the highly educated Mugabe has become in some way the new oppressor to Zimbabweans in his repressive ways of responding to political opponents (Godwin, 2011; Holland, 2010; Meredith, 2007. Cracking down on civilians to stay in power, as he has done, replicates the oppressive practices of slavery and the colonial era.

During slavery, the slave masters would whip slaves that revolted against them or were captured while trying to escape. In the so-called postcolonial and postslavery era, we have witnessed many Black leaders, like Mugabe, doing similar things, such as illegally and forcefully putting dissidents in jail with impunity. Mugabe's government has also been accused of sending paramilitary groups to crack down on people who oppose his government (Godwin, 2011; Holland, 2010). As a case in point, during the presidential election in 2007, his opponent, Morgan Tsvangirai, accused Mugabe of sending special armed forces to physically attack him. Tsvangirai appeared on public television with bruises on his face and arms to denounce this physical attack against him. Mugabe tried to refute his opponent's accusation but could not provide a convincing argument. The bruises on Morgan Tsvangirai's face were undeniable evidence that Mugabe did use physical force against his opponent to stay in power as many dictators have done throughout history. Despite his political rhetoric of change, Mugabe has unfortunately proven to be an oppressor throughout the decades he has been in power.

How About Obama, the "Postcolonial" and "Postslavery" American President?

Another "postcolonial" president whose political actions, in terms of both his domestic and foreign policies, deserve analytical attention here is Barack Obama. At the outset, it is worth acknowledging some basic differences and similarities between Obama and African leaders alluded to earlier. For example, Obama does not crack down on civilians to stay in power like Mugabe has, perhaps because the current US political context in which he has been operating has not compelled him to do so. However, like Mugabe, Obama turns his back on groups of people for whom he should have shown some compassion but has not shown any. For example, Obama's record on deportation of immigrants of color has surpassed that of his White predecessors, even though his father was a Black immigrant man from Kenya (Gonzales, 2013; Nicholls, 2013). Moreover, as a former community organizer in Chicago, Obama must have had interacted with immigrants of color and/ or children of immigrant parents of color, for Chicago is a city with a great number of immigrants of color. Yet, since elected in 2008, he has not done much to solve the legal situation of immigrants of color in this country. His immigration policy has worsened the socioeconomic, social, and educational situations of undocumented immigrants and their families. Needless to say, Obama's position on the immigration issue has been very disappointing. There is no reason to hope he will change his position on this crucial issue, as he is now toward the end of his second term. In short, as the son of an African immigrant, and a former community organizer working in poor communities of color, his unprecedented deportation record of poor immigrants of color is nothing but a disgrace.

Obama's foreign policy is equally disappointing. In complicity with European imperialist powers including France and the UK, Obama's government participated in the political destabilization of Libya, leading to the overthrow and murder of an African leader, Moammar Khadafi (Chomsky, 2014). Specifically, Obama allied with White European leaders, such as the British prime minister, David Cameron, and the former French president, Nicolas Sarkozy, to overthrow (for geopolitical interests) an African leader whom many people, particularly Africans, saw as their hero. Not only did Obama and his White European presidents overthrow and contributed to the death of Khadafi but they also divided, destabilized, and destroyed the country. Chomsky (2014) states,

> In March 2011, amid an Arab Spring uprising against Libyan ruler Moammar Gadhafi, the U.N. Security Council passed Resolution 1973, calling for "a cease-fire and a complete end to violence and all attacks against, and abuses of civilians." The imperial triumvirate—France, England, the US—instantly chose to violate the Resolution, becoming the air force of the rebels and sharply enhancing violence. Their campaign culminated in the assault on Gadhafi's refuge in Sirte, which they left "utterly ravaged," "reminiscent of the grimmest scenes from Grozny, towards the end of Russia's bloody Chechen war," according to eyewitness reports in the British press. At a bloody cost, the triumvirate accomplished its goal of regime change in violation of pious pronouncements to the contrary (p. 2).

In addition to deporting immigrants of color and participating in the murder of Khadafi, Obama has authorized the use of drone strikes leading to the murder of Third World people in countries like Pakistan, Afghanistan, and Somalia (Benjamin, 2013; Scahill, 2013; Clarke, 2014). It seems the White power structure that Obama inherited has psychologized him to the point where he has become as oppressive as his White predecessors, like George Bush and Ronald Reagan, who used the same violent, inhumane, and imperialist strategies to fight the so-called enemy abroad. In the name of safety, self-defense, and national security interest, President Obama, like his White predecessors, has become an imperialist warmonger killing poor people of color abroad. Killing innocent people through drone strikes will be part of Obama's political legacy.

Furthermore, as a man of color, Obama must have experienced various forms of racism, regardless of his social class. Yet, his approach on race issue seems to have been more about pleasing White liberals and conservatives, rather than taking a firm position aimed at challeng-ing the unfair and inequitable nature of the *racial contract* shaping the United States' political and economic structure (Mills, 1997). In other words, his presidency as the first president of color has not contributed much, if anything, to the struggle against White supremacy. On the contrary, racist individuals have used Obama's presidency as a green light to murder young Black men with impunity, like Trayvon Martin's and Jordan Davis' murder cases illuminate. These cases of racial murder will most likely continue to occur after Obama completes his second term as president. His legacy will most likely be used as a proxy to dis-regard or justify the poor living conditions of Blacks and other people of color under the pretext that they are lazy if they do not succeed as Obama did.

As noted in the first chapter, Obama must be given credit for taking a political stance for the rights of women and members of the LBGTQ community. However, as far as race and class equality issues are con-cerned, it is unlikely that he will be remembered as the "change you can believe in" president he proclaimed to be while campaigning for president. Most people Obama has appointed to key political positions have been mostly White males—including conservative White males like Larry Summer—who have been pimping the political system for decades for their own political and professional success. As Obama completes his second term, most of his appointees are still conservative, corporate White males who served in previous governments. Hence, it will be foolish to think his government will effect any fundamental change within the US political system.

The examples of Barack Obama, Mobutu Sese Seko, Joseph Mug-abe, and Blaise Compaoré used here are only a few among many. How-ever, the point that ought to be made is the following: because some Black or Brown people are elected as presidents or appointed as prime ministers in many formerly colonized countries or imperialist coun-tries, like the United States, does not necessarily mean that their pres-idency will lead to the transformation of the colonial rule or White supremacist system. Like colonialism, racism is systemic. The fact that the colonizers left or were forced to leave does not mean that the colonial seed planted in the colonized land automatically disappeared.

Had this been the case, former colonial powers would not have had economic and political influence or control over former colonies decades or even centuries after they left. History has proven that many formerly colonized countries continue to be dependent on their former colonial power to survive economically and politically.

With regard to Obama's presidency and legacy in particular, it was an illusion (and still is in the mind of many Americans) to believe that Obama as the first African American president would solve the racial, socioeconomic problems that minorities and poor Whites have been facing in the United States for centuries. Oppressive systems like White supremacy and racism do not disappear overnight. These statements are in no way to be interpreted as a cover-up for Obama's government, that is, to justify Obama's silence and passivity on racial and economic inequality in the United States. Obama, surrounded by people belonging to the same White male club for centuries, has not proven to be courageous enough to take bold actions aimed at agitating the White supremacist political system—and maybe he never will. This system has been run for centuries by conservative, corporate White males, who too often have been oblivious to social inequality facing historically marginalized groups.

White Supremacy and US Imperialism in the Age of Obama's America

The persistence of White supremacy in this country has led to the oppression and impoverishment of African Americans, Native Americans, Latino/as, Blacks, Asians, immigrants of color, and other oppressed groups. Yet, the postracial discourse, emerging particularly after Barack Obama was elected and reelected as the first Black president in the United States in 2008 and 2012, respectively, has continued to be used as a cover-up to mask the increasing inequitable racial, socioeconomic, and educational conditions facing people of color, particularly African Americans, Native Americans, and Latino/as living in this country. A handful of rich and famous people of color, namely President Barack Obama and former US secretaries of state, Colin Powell and Condoleezza Rice, and Supreme Court Justice Clarence Thomas, might be exempt from the savage forms of racism to which ordinary, poor people of color have been subjected. These political African American figures are highly successful Blacks trapped in a Black or Brown skin but operate from a White dominant ideology mindset. Their colonized, submissive behaviors and deferential attitude toward the White establishment seem to have contributed to its perpetuation.

For example, Justice Clarence Thomas has not taken a position supporting Black initiatives, programs, or organizations. For instance, he has opposed affirmative action, which has enabled people of color, particularly African Americans, to attend universities and colleges that would have been closed to them otherwise; to work at certain places that would have been closed to them; and to have access to certain state and federal programs and benefits that were denied to them. Affirmative action has led to some form of restorative racial justice for African Americans, Native Americans, and Latino/as. Historically, these groups have been disproportionately discriminated against in American society.

To maintain the White status quo, the architects of White supremacy in the United States have allowed a few tokenized Blacks to climb the White political ladder, grooming and promoting them politically, like President Barack Obama. Meanwhile, the conditions for people of color (particularly those who are poor) and poor Whites are getting worse every day. Given horrendous forms of racism to which people of color, particularly people of African descent, have been subjected, it is worth asking if the novel idea of freedom and pursuit of happiness for which the founding fathers of this country fought applies to these historically oppressed groups.

The founding fathers did not consider Black and Brown people to be human enough to be part of the social contract that they envisioned all Americans would benefit from. The legacy of racism and the wide spread of White supremacist ideology, which shaped the institutional structure—including the legal, economic, and school systems—and the political landscape of this country confirm this assertion. For instance, Native Americans, African Americans, Latino/as, Asians, and immigrants of color have been historically subjected to savage forms of racism, such as being lynched, being unjustly incarcerated, being placed in internment camps or boarding schools, being chased by dogs, and being brutally beaten like animals by police officers. Although some progress has been made—such as in the case of African Americans, who are now allowed to vote (although with some severe restrictions in some states like Florida) eat in the same restaurants as Whites, and attend racially integrated schools—racism persists.

Racism has taken different forms and shapes depending on the era. During slavery and the Jim Crow era, Blacks were lynched by racist mobs like the Ku Klux Klan. Nowadays, they may not be brutally lynched and hung by the Klan, but they have been victims of a legal system that has given license to police officers to unfairly arrest them, brutalize them, put them in jail for minor offenses, or, worse yet, murder them with impunity. As Alexander (2010) cogently points out in her book, *The New Jim Crow*, many racialized minorities have been massively incarcerated for either crimes they never committed or for minor offenses for which Whites (particularly affluent Whites) would not be punished. Specifically, Alexander explains how the legal system has stigmatized and condemned former inmates to a life of despair and hopelessness, preventing them from obtaining employment, housing, quality health care, and education. She states, "we have not ended racial caste in America; we have merely redesigned it" (Alexander, 2010, p. 81). She goes further to state that "More African Americans are under correctional control today . . . than were enslaved in 1850" (p. 82). Alexander's book uncovers the myth that the United States has entered a postracial era with the election and reelection of Barack Obama.

Obama's presidency has been used as a sociopolitical tool aimed at masking the horrific racial, educational, and socioeconomic conditions of Black and Brown people. Likewise, his legacy will most likely be used as an ideological strategy and racial symbol by White supremacist groups and the mainstream media to cover up the misery of African Americans, Blacks, Native Americans, Latino/as, Chicano/as, and Asians. Obama will be remembered as merely a friendlier face of the US neocolonial and imperialist, oppressive power, unless he changes his policies that have had disastrous effects on the poor and the vulnerable. Neither his presidency nor his legacy will stop the continued effects of racism and White supremacy on the lives of people of color, whose socioeconomic and educational conditions have gotten worse.

Given all this, it is worth asking if Obama's victory was not part of a larger political conspiracy. Specifically, one must ask whether Obama was allowed to be elected as president so that dominant groups in society could further perpetuate the color-blindness ideology that has been circulated in school and the media, making people believe that Whites are not racist anymore because they voted for a Black man. Such a discourse fundamentally aims at making people, both Whites and non-Whites, accept the White status quo.

Obama's presidency did not, and his legacy will not, protect Black and Brown people, particularly the poor, from continuing to be victims of White supremacy and institutional racism. Since Obama was elected in 2008 and reelected in 2012, White supremacist groups have been more visible than before, and many innocent Black and Brown men and women have been victims of hate crimes committed by racist police officers and individual Whites, like the Trayvon Martin, Michael Brown, and Ramarley Graham murder cases demonstrate. Similar murders will most likely continue to occur unless transformative structural changes occur in this country at all levels—personal, political, legal, economical, educational, and cultural. As it stands now, the racially biased US legal system, combined with the White supremacist ideology that has fed it, have led many White individuals and police officers to believe that they can murder Black and Brown people and go unpunished. Unfortunately, this has repeatedly happened.

Conclusion

As discussed throughout this chapter in particular, and the book in general, the internalization of White supremacist ideology has deeply affected people of color in many ways and on many levels. Specifically, the internalization of this ideology influences the perception, the behavior, and actions of many people of color, including President Barack Obama. Like Whites, people of color who internalize White supremacist ideology often act upon socially constructed racial stereotypes and stigmas about other people of color, and their actions and behavior at times reflect those of White oppressors, White masters. Indoctrination and internalization of White dominant ideology has prevented many other people of color from uniting with other people of color to challenge White supremacy. Unless political leaders of color, like President Obama and African leaders noted earlier, engage in the process of decolonizing their minds (Thiong'o, 1986) and adopting an anti–White supremacist, anticolonial mindset and attitude, and taking actions aimed at resisting White hegemonic ideology, their day of mental liberation and freedom might not ever come. Their legacy will be tainted with colonized behaviors and oppressive actions similar to those of former European colonizers and White masters, and President Obama is no exception.

5
RACE, CLASS, AND POWER
Obama Caught in Sergeant Crowley
and Professor Gates' Racial Controversy

The Abysmal State of Race Relations in American culture is a coming source of bewilderment and frustration. The reappearance of overt racist activity, especially on college and secondary campuses, forces us to reevaluate our understanding of race as we approach the last decade of the twentieth century. In particular, the liberal theory of race, which has dominated the American understanding of race relations, has exhibited a crisis of explanation, manifested in its exponents' inability to elucidate persistent forms of Afro-American oppression.

(Dyson, 2004, p. 37)

Race is the most explosive in American life precisely because it forces us to confront the tragic facts of poverty and paranoia, despair and distrust. In short, a candid examination of race matters takes us to the core of the crisis of American democracy. And the degree to which race matters in the plight and predicament of fellow citizens is a crucial measure of whether we can keep alive the best of this democratic experiment we call America.

(West, 1993, p. 156)

Introduction

This chapter examines Obama's involvement in Professor Henry Louis Gates' and Sergeant James Crowley's racial controversy, which occurred in 2009. While browsing the Internet to look for international news,

I came across breaking news about Professor Henry Louis Gates' arrest by Sergeant James Crowley. My first reaction was: This could have happened to me as a Black man living in the United States, a country that takes pride in its democratic principles, even though its legal system has not been functional for many people, particularly those born with the "wrong skin tone" and from the "wrong" racial, socioeconomic, sexual, and religious backgrounds. The information available to the public suggests that Sergeant Crowley responded to a call from a woman who reported a possible house break-in by two men.

According to the 911 tapes, a woman said that she saw two men with suitcases on the porch of the house where Professor Gates lives. She also said that one of the men could have been Hispanic but she was not sure. As the police officer, Crowley, was trying to locate the suspected burglars, he stepped onto the porch of the house where Professor Gates lives, knocked on his door, and asked him to step out. Professor Gates apparently resisted as he felt that he did not do anything wrong. Upon the police officer's request, Professor Gates showed him his identification card and his proof of residence. Apparently, Sergeant Crowley and Professor Gates exchanged words, and the latter was arrested for "disorderly conduct." Being arrested for "disorderly conduct" might sound familiar to many Blacks, Latino/as, Native Americans, and other marginalized and racially targeted groups in this country. When such groups attempt to challenge officers who are racially profiling them—violating their civil and human rights—they are often accused of being violent, which is usually, if not always, used as a pretext by these police officers to arrest and brutalize them.

Many Black and Brown men and women have been physically and psychologically brutalized by police officers, particularly White police officers, who may feel threatened by these Black and Brown men and women. Rodney King, who was savagely beaten by several police officers in Los Angeles in 1992 for supposedly resisting police arrest and being violent to those officers, is a classic example. Of course, countless similar examples can be given. By contrast, cases of police brutality against White men are scarce. It is as if no White male has ever challenged the authority of a White police officer when he feels that this officer is abusing his power. Further, it seems that, unlike Black and Brown men, White men have not been arrested and brutalized by White police officers because they are not violent. I am not suggesting that there are not any violent Black and Brown men, because there are. But there are also violent White men. Why is it then that the percentage of Black and Brown men who have been arrested by police officers and ended up being incarcerated is a lot higher than that of White men?

Many White police officers have racially profiled, brutalized, and even murdered Black/Brown men under the pretext that they were "violent and aggressive." Did Amadou Diallo and Sean Bell, among others, show any sign of violence towards the police officers who murdered them? Was I violent toward the police officer who pulled me over and arrested me for no apparent reason while I was on my way home from school in 1994? This White police officer followed me as if I had committed a crime. When he finally found an excuse to stop me, he asked me why my eyes were red. I was not sure what he meant by that, so I responded by saying, "That is the natural color of my eyes and that if you find them more red than normal it could be because I am tired after a long day at school." The police officer said, "I worked all day too, and my eyes are not red." As an immigrant who did not know exactly what my rights were, I was scared to death when the police arrested me. This police officer could not give my brother a valid reason as to why he arrested me. When my brother came to bail me out the same day, the police officer told him that he arrested me because I was speeding. Unsatisfied with the officer's response, my brother said, "You arrested him because he was speeding?" The officer then augmented his story saying that "The main reason for your brother's arrest is that he stopped in the wrong lane when I asked him to pull over." However, the police officer had not mentioned this reason to me when he proceeded to arrest me.

With regard to Professor Gates, let us presume that he overreacted and possibly questioned Sergeant Crowley's authority by asking him to show him his police badge number. Let us assume that Professor Gates was very upset and, therefore, expressed his anger as he was talking to the police officer. Did he not have the right to do so after being racially targeted and asked to step outside in order to be interrogated about something he was not even aware of? Does not one have the right to be assertive when one feels that his or her human and civil rights have been violated? How could he be arrested after he showed Sergeant Crowley his Harvard identification card and established that he lived in that house? Why did not Sergeant Crowley trust what Professor Gates told him and apologize for invading his space and privacy? Apologizing to an innocent Black man who has been racially harassed and, in many cases, physically beaten has been difficult for many White police officers. We witnessed this in many racial profiling and police brutality cases such as Abner Louima, the Haitian immigrant who was brutally sodomized with a broken broomstick by several New York police officers.

I was not present for that incident in Cambridge. Therefore, it is impossible for me to know all the details. However, given the history of racial profiling against men of African descent, Latino/as, Native Americans, and other targeted groups such as people from the Middle East, I am inclined to believe that race was the determining factor in Professor Gates' arrest and humiliation. What happened to Professor Gates could have happened to me or to any other Black or Brown man living in this country. In fact, this is happening to Black and Brown men every day here in the United States. The only difference between Professor Gates' case and those of other Black men who have been harassed by police officers, particularly White police officers, is that Gates is a highly respected professor at one of the most prestigious universities in the world. This was arguably one of the reasons Professor Gates was invited to the White House to share "a beer with the president" with the expectation of finding ways to make peace with Sergeant Crowley, who had racially profiled him. Poor Black males who have been victims of racial profiling do not receive the treatment that Professor Gates received. Class matters: had Professor Gates been a Black or Brown janitor, most likely this racial profiling case would not have gotten the national and international media attention it did. Furthermore, a janitor most likely would not have been released as quickly as Professor Gates was, and it is unlikely President Barack Obama would have been involved in this highly publicized racial profiling.

Unpacking Race, Class, and Power: Obama vs. Sergeant Crowley's and Gates' Racial Storm

Commenting on Sergeant Crowley's and Professor Henry Louis Gates' racial controversy in 2009, President Obama stated that the police officer "acted stupidly" in arresting Professor Gates the way he did.

Soon after, under political pressure President Obama apologized for his statement. President Obama may have withdrawn his statement because he was afraid of being attacked and called a racist by Whites. Not only did he take his statement back, but he also invited Sergeant Crowley and Professor Gates to the White House to share a beer with him in an effort to alleviate the situation. However, the questions remain: Would the president be willing to do the same for other ordinary Black and Brown men who are, as I am writing this chapter, being racially profiled and brutalized by White police officers? Thus, in analyzing Professor Gates and Sergeant Crowley's situation it can be argued that in this case race and class play an important role in the way the American public perceived, understood or interpreted this highly publicized racial profiling case.

While inviting Professor Gates and Sergeant Crowley to have a beer at the White House to discuss the racial incident might have appeased the anger of many Whites, particularly that of Sergeant Crowley and his family, this symbolic action did not and will not solve anything as far as the racial division in this country is concerned. Nor will this gesture help end racial profiling. This system, which is endemically racist, needs to be radically changed through racial and social *conscientization* (Freire, 1970) and praxis by Black and Brown people, and White allies. However "regrettable" this may be for the Cambridge Police Department and however upsetting and outrageous it may be for many people of color in this country, the racial controversy in this case once more confirms that Black and Brown men are not safe anywhere in this country as long as institutional racism and White supremacy persist. By virtue of merely being a Black or Brown person, one is subject to ill treatment regardless of his or her level of education and social status, as in the case of Professor Gates. Unless some serious structural change occurs in the US legal system, achieving racial and economic equality will remain a dream. The lady who called to report the possible house break-in said in a public statement that her parents have always taught her to judge people based on their character but not on their skin color. What she said certainly sounds beautiful, but one must question whether or not she would have called the police if she had seen two White men "breaking into" someone's house.

Regardless of many individual Whites' good intentions, many continue to see people of color through a racial lens, and often act on their vision in ways that are detrimental to Black/Brown people's lives. Given the racial oppression to which professional Black and Brown people have been subjugated, one must ask the following questions: Should professional Black and Brown people bear a sign on their Black and Brown face or forehead saying, "I am a university professor, I am a doctor, a lawyer, or, in brief, I am a professional" in order to be respected and free from racial profiling? Would this strategy prevent them from being racially profiled? Why should Black and Brown men and women have to do this anyway? Why can't they be treated equally regardless of their skin tone? How can we talk about human rights, democracy, justice, freedom, and pursuit of happiness in this country when certain groups of people are racially profiled every day and discriminated against almost everywhere they go, whether it be at the store, the supermarket, at work, or on college and university campuses? Should we conclude that this country is a very hypocritical nation with a legal system that works mostly for those who are White and wealthy?

All socioeconomic and political indicators suggest that Black and Brown men's image has been distorted. The historical misrepresentation of Black men from slavery onward continues to be the determining factor that often—if not always—leads to their poor treatment in society. Even though slavery has been outlawed, its legacy continues to haunt men and women of African descent like a shadow. It is unquestionable that other forms of racial, socioeconomic, and political oppression have emerged after slavery.

However, many of these forms of oppression are rooted in the ever-present legacy of slavery; they have simply been masked under different names. It is sometimes argued that colonization is a thing of the past, but it has been revitalized by Western occupation of other lands and to a great extent by a Western form of globalization. If this were not the case, countless Black and Brown men and women here and abroad would not continue to suffer economically, politically, socially, and educationally. This argument about the persistent effect of colonization and slavery on people of African descent and others has been contested by many so-called Western Marxists; many of whom happen to be White males.

For instance, when providing feedback on a manuscript in which I argued that the legacy of slavery and colonization continues to negatively impact the subjectivity and material conditions of Black and Brown men of African descent, a White male editor who is a self-proclaimed Marxist commented, "Despite some efforts on your part to avoid this impression, the essay reads like a kind of progressive Moynihanism: privileged Whites, from slave owners to the contemporary straight middle class, have fucked up Black subjectivity, which is, well, pretty fucked up." This editor admitted that he did not finish reading the whole manuscript. He stated that he got through half of it and disliked it enough to stop reading it. When I asked him what parts of the article were not substantiated, he could not tell. This editor apparently was unwilling to question his White privilege. Further, he seemed to be triggered by my uncompromising position on and analysis of the harmful effect of the legacy of slavery and racism on Black/Brown men's subjective and material conditions.

Racial Profiling and Institutional Racism

Like many university professors, sometimes I go to my office on the weekends to write. The building is usually empty, especially when school is not in session. I sometimes stay late in my office. Given the history of racial profiling against Black/Brown male professors on campus by the university police, I always fear that one day I might be racially targeted as a possible burglar. Therefore, I always carry my university card and other items that I can use as evidence in the event the university police should stop and interrogate me. There were a few times when I forgot my university identification card, and I suddenly panicked and rushed back home to get it. Reflecting the next day on this, I asked myself: Why does a human being have to experience this feeling in a country that calls itself democratic and which has forcibly exported and imposed its "form of democracy package" on other countries?

After Professor Gates' and other Black and Brown professors' racial profiling on college and university campuses, I have become even more fearful when working in my office on the weekends. My office on the weekends does not feel like a space where I, as a university professor, can peacefully and comfortably sit to do my academic work. However, like many tenure-track professors, I am pressured to publish or perish—let alone fulfilling other academic obligations, such as teaching, presenting papers at conferences, serving on committees and attending departmental meetings. In addition to fighting against the negative effect of a corporate model of education that has shaped many universities, progressive professors of color have to cope regularly with racial harassment from university police officers and other racist individuals. When professors of color take a stance against racial profiling and harassment at their university, they are often labeled as angry people and/or bad team players and complainers (Stanley, 2006).

However, as an associate professor I have not yet experienced this type of racial harassment, profiling, and name calling. While I was a doctoral student at a major university located in western Massachusetts, I did experience racial profiling on campus, and I felt isolated as some seemingly racially prejudice professors did not seem to share my ideology and strong stance on racial issues. Nonetheless, with self-determination, hard work, persistence, and support from some caring faculty members, I was able to complete my doctoral degree.

Racism has been challenging for people of color not only in this country but also in the world. For example, what happened to Professor Gates in Cambridge, Massachusetts, could have happened to him in Latin America, Europe, Asia, and even in communities of color. Like many Whites, many people of color have internalized stereotypes about other people of color, although perhaps not to the same extent as Whites. As a case in point, people of color have called on and reported other people of color to the police out of "Black fear" that they have learned and internalized. This is a direct effect of White supremacist groups' strategic plan to divide and conquer.

Unfortunately, many Black and White people's perceptions and actions have been shaped and informed by this awful plan. Being Black or Brown is a shadow that has been following Black and Brown people wherever they happen to be, irrespective of their social class and achievements. One's Black and Brown face is the racial marker that many individuals base their judgment on when they place a Black/Brown person in the "violent, lazy, savage, and stupid" box. Blacks and other racially marginalized groups have been historically constructed through this lens for centuries, especially by those in power, who have labeled, isolated, and oppressed Black and Brown people. Needless to say, blackness is seen as a pejorative racial marker while whiteness is seen as *the* standard.

However, with the ascendance of Barack Obama to the presidency, many people, including Whites, naïvely assumed that he would bridge the racial gap between Whites and non-Whites. Likewise, political pundits referred to Obama's victory to claim that race does not or should not matter because we have a Black president. Still others believed that Obama would positively restore the image of Black people not only in the United States but also in the world. Refuting these claims, I argue that having a Black president, surrounded by almost the same conservative and so-called White liberals (mostly males) who have been benefiting from the political system for decades, will not change such a system and bring about racial and socioeconomic justice for all. It was and still is unrealistic to expect President Obama to reverse a racist system that has been oppressive to people of color for centuries. President Obama could have collaborated with progressives to start creating the foundation of a solid path towards racial and economic justice, among others. Perhaps this is too much to expect of a first Black president lading a country that has been historically and politically dominated by Whites, particularly conservative, wealthy Whites.

Conclusion

Obama's involvement in the racial storm stemming from Sergeant Crowley's and Professor Henry Louis Gates' controversy was merely a political gesture. More specifically, inviting a White police officer and a Black male, who was victim of racial profiling, to the White House to have a beer with the president was nothing but political symbolism. We need to go beyond political symbolism to take concrete steps tackling various types of racial problems that the United States and other countries around the world have been grappling with. Until we are all—Black, Brown and White people—willing to face race courageously and honestly talk about it (the signifier that haunts the mind and psyche of many people across the racial line)—we will remain a nation of cowards sunk in deep racial denial.

6
BEYOND OBAMA'S HISTORICAL SYMBOLISM

Pierre W. Orelus and Eduardo
Bonilla-Silva in Dialogue

The Obama victory will be of great assistance in waging the struggle for racial justice. But electoral politics is not a substitute for social protest organizing in neighborhoods and in the streets.

(Marable, as cited in Russell Rickford, 2011, p. 232)

This dialogue between myself and Professor Eduardo Bonilla-Silva took place on September 18, 2008, two months before Obama was elected as president. In this dialogue, we critically examine the ways in which institutional racism has impacted the subjective and material conditions of people of color, particularly men of color. We further analyze the extent to which Black masculinity has been historically misrepresented. We then point out how the misrepresentation of men of color has led to their stigmatization and ill treatment in society. Professors Bonilla-Silva and Orelus question Obama's stance on race and class issues in the context of the United States, predicting that his presidency will not lead to the betterment of socioeconomic conditions of poor Black and Brown people. Professor Bonilla-Silva states that, for example, Obama, a Black man, will be "a symbol for White people." Unfortunately, Bonilla-Silva's prediction about Obama's presidency and legacy has proven to be accurate, as illuminated through the analysis of effects of Obama's domestic and foreign policies.

Orelus: What does it mean to be a Black man in this country or, for that matter, in the world?

Bonilla-Silva: Blackness changes depending on your location. You are from the Caribbean. As you know, in many Caribbean nations and actually in many countries in the world blackness is contested because our identity as Black people is sort of sanctioned within a nationalistic discourse. In such places, making a game of blackness is a common thing because in a way you are viewed as ruining the nation, dividing the nation, dividing the people who are presumably united by the nation. Now what that does is hide the history of racial oppression. It's just a new, a different form of organizing the racial structures of these countries. We know that our notion of blackness changes depending on context, so it's not by chance that many Blacks particularly from the Hispanic Caribbean become extremely race conscious when they switch boats; it's more so for Blacks from Puerto Rico, Cuba, Colombia, Republican Dominic, Venezuela, Mexico, to places like the US.

Again, this does not mean that we don't have a racial structure in Puerto Rico, Cuba, etc. It means that blackness is differently structured; therefore, the space to recognize blackness and to develop a Black consciousness is much harder in those places. If you allow me to use the concept of Marx in relation to race, in the Americas we are a race *in* itself without being a race *for* itself. We need to recognize that we are treated differently here, that we are regarded differently, and that there is a space to recognize our blackness; therefore, here we become racially conscious and aware.

Orelus: So let me ask you a follow-up question on this issue. Do you believe that the ongoing effect of slavery and colonialism has something to do with the way people of color, especially Black men, have been treated?

Bonilla-Silva: Yes, but I also want to add that obviously it is not just because of the history of slavery and colonialism. All history produced racial structures that have continued to remain in place. These structures are different depending on the country but they exist nonetheless. Let me explain. In many countries including the US, the way of avoiding dealing with the race question today is to make the claim that racism was something really bad that we had in the past because of slavery.

In the case of the US slavery, and Jim Crow, we claim that slavery was bad, but after it was abolished that was the end of racism. I want to argue that that's not the case because in all the Caribbean and the Americas after the abolition of slavery, we were somewhat metamorphosed into a different racial order. Today a hundred and plus years after the abolition of slavery in our countries, we still have a racial order, differently structured, but a racial order nonetheless. Therefore, our continued struggle for the recognition of our identity and equality is not just a struggle based on legacies but it is a struggle based on contemporary structure of racism.

Orelus: So are you saying that slavery does have an effect on the way we have been treated as Black people, that the way this system is structured does not allow Black people to come to voice? In other words, we continue being a victim of the history of slavery.

Bonilla-Silva: I am saying more than that. I am saying that fundamentally the mere abolition of slavery was not the end of racial order. The abolition of slavery led the world to a new racial order. We don't need to revisit history. The point is that the abolition of slavery did not lead to equality; it simply led to a different system of subordination that lasted in most places over a hundred years. For example, I just came from a trip to the island of Bermuda. Just to share with you an interesting fact, Black folks who represent the majority of the population there were not allowed to have one man, one vote until 1968; so this means that even though slavery was abolished in the nineteenth century, they had legal second-class citizens until that day. Then from 1968 onward they still have a second-class citizen social status. Even though now they have what the White folks call Black power, which means they control the governmental apparatus, they don't control the economy. Therefore, as you know, if you don't control the economy, controlling politics is nothing.

Orelus: Are we experiencing a new form of colonialism?

Bonilla-Silva: There is a new form of oppression. We can call it *neocolonialism*, which is a contemporary version of colonialism. We can call it many ways, or use whatever terms you want to use. Colonial or racial domination did not end with the abolition of slavery; it was just metamorphosed and that is not typical only of the Caribbean but also of the Black folks in the US, who are not oppressed today just because of the effects of slavery, but they are also oppressed because there are new ways of reproducing White privilege and White supremacy.

Orelus: The battle against the misrepresentation of people of color, particularly the dark-skinned ones, through the mass corporate media, schools, and even churches, is a perpetual battle. How would you suggest that we fight in a way that would not lead to the perpetuation of negative stereotypes against us?

Bonilla-Silva: I am doing some work on that subject right now. A lot of our struggle is based on the assumption of rationality, that is on the assumption that if we just convince White folks of the folly of their thinking, we will be able to overcome as the civil rights movement tried to do. The problem with that assumption is something that I call in my work a *racial grammar* that started 500 years ago when we invented this category of race that's being produced and reproduced for 500 years; that's an organized cognition and even emotion, "I am one of us."

That racial grammar will never allow the facts of race to be interpreted the way we think it should be interpreted by Whites. For example, we provide the data on the unemployment of Black people in the Americas. White people interpret it as, "you are unemployed because you are lazy." We provide the data on the overrepresentation of Black people in the penal system. White people interpret that as, "because you're violent." You provide data on Blacks of lesser income and lesser education, and White people interpret that as "of course because you are stupid." Therefore, what I am suggesting to do is following a lot of the Caribbean thinkers like Fanon and others.

All intellectuals, like Bob Marley said, need to begin a process of the emancipation from mental slavery. For this, although we welcome progressive Whites as our allies, we need not depend on them; we have to begin fighting, no matter what and no matter where; it is a combination of a progressive nationalist stand. We can't hide our own sense of history, sense of self, of practice and logic; we don't have to continue the assumption that we have to use their ideas to free ourselves. In this process obviously, the central element will always be the same that we have always used forever, that is struggle. We need to continue to struggle. By this I mean social movement politics, rather than this foolishness of believing in electoral politics.

For example, with regard the Obama phenomenon, the assumption is that by voting in an election we are going to free ourselves. It's an illusion. Unlike the US where there had never been a Black person in charge, we who are from the Caribbean, because of our history and our struggle, have learned the hard way that leaders should be judged not by the color of their skin, but by the content of their politics. Therefore, I don't care to have a Black leader if the position of that leader happens to be reactionary.

If my Black leader claims that he wants to have a thousand more people in the military, I am not happy with that; if my Black leader is for espionage, I don't like that Black leader. If my Black leader tells me that he basically wants to follow the same politics that the US has followed in Palestine, I don't want that Black leader. Our liberation should come from struggle, from politics in social movement, and from organization, rather than from hoping to convince (which is what Obama has been trying to do) White folks that he is a soft Negro that they can trust and one that will not raise hell in the racial front.

Orelus: Obama has been getting both national and international attention perhaps because of his racial hybridity, but certainty because of his charisma and what he represents, or rather because of how he is being represented through the mainstream media. Do you believe Obama will be able to deliver what he has been promising to people throughout his campaign, or do you think he has just been allowed to perform on a show put together by White hegemonic, dominant, and Christian men?

Bonilla-Silva: Absolutely! The way he has shaped his politics and policies and his persona in every occasion is by reminding his audience that his mother is White and his father is not from the US but from Africa. In the US his blackness, his ethnic blackness, is more tolerable for Whites than blackness from the US. If his father were a Black man from the southern side of Chicago, his hybridity would be more of a problem than it already is. Furthermore, he has avoided using the term *racism* in his campaign. Actually the only time that he used it was to chastise Reverend Wright who claimed that racism was endemic.

However, according to Obama, it (racism) has not been endemic in America, which suggests that Reverend Wright is crazy. He has obviously made a color-blind appeal, a nationalistic appeal by saying so. Obama is famous for saying, "I don't see a Black America, I don't see a White America, I only see the United States of America." He needs to go to an eye doctor and get some new glasses so he can see the White America, the Black America, and the Latino/a America, etc. I don't think that he would help us with the racial divide, because the racial divide is not based on a misunderstanding; the racial divide is based on inequality. What you need to have is policies that address the root causes of inequality among racial groups as well as a policy of reparation. None of that is in the agenda of Obama. Therefore, what you are going to get is a symbol—Obama, a Black man, a symbol for White people. This would mean we are finally over race because we have a Black president. For Black people, on the other hand, it would be a short lead symbol of possibilities.

Black people have put their emotions, their aspirations in this Black man, but people don't need emotions or aspirations. After a few years of having Obama as president leading in the same conditions, they will mimic the commercial and ask, "President Obama, where's the beef?"

Orelus: Maleness as an identity is fluid. Let's take the example of a Black man who was born and grew up in a White neighborhood, who went to a school predominantly attended by White students, and who mostly interacted with White men and women. This Black man might perform his maleness differently than a Black man who was born and grew up in a predominantly Black community.

How do you think Obama has performed his maleness publically and politically?

Bonilla-Silva: Obviously, this is a complex matter, so I might not have all the answers. But blackness is unstable, it is always contested as well as masculinity. And as you suggested, it is connected to class position and context; based on what I've learned from people who know him, Obama has different performances of masculinity. For example, because he doesn't want to raise hell, in the campaign he has to keep a soft masculinity, almost a feminine approach. For example, he is chastised, called names, and he never fights back. But most Black men from a working-class background would be in the business of kicking ass, in the business of fighting back, in the business of defending the sexist notion, and, to use the sexist notion, in the business of defending manhood.

Obama, who has performed an almost feminine public persona and performance for mostly White audiences, apparently has a different persona when he is with his people. If you, for example, go to *YouTube* and see some of his speeches before Black audiences, he really switches from so-called Standard English to an English that is closer to the so-called Black English. He is more sort of a *homie* in his style. He is always suave. Maybe that is part of his persona, but it is a different performance of his masculinity.

For all of us, I guess that our class and the context determine how we perform masculinity. Presumably, you and I as professors, we should perform a softer version of masculinity that is non-threatening to our colleagues. I only play that game, but I don't give any corners to White folks; I do it as I see it, and I say it as I do it, so I don't give corners; I don't change my performance whether I am with Whites or Black folks. White people get a lot of color from me.

Orelus: Do you see any connection between blackness and masculinity? In other words, do you think that the way Black men behave is related to their blackness, their racial identity?

Bonilla-Silva: I haven't thought much about this connection between masculinity, gender identity and performance, and racial identity and performance. I do think that for people who have been put down, (I am talking about men, so for women such views may be somewhat different) for Black men who have been ostracized, literally castrated so on and so forth, I understand why in some segments of the population the version of masculinity takes the form of a hyper-masculinity. When you are put down, you can chose to either die or fight back by being accessibly masculine; this approach is somewhat connected to racial oppression. For the middle-class folks such as Colin Powell (besides Obama) who want to mimic Whiteness so as to achieve mobility, you have another version of masculinity, a softer-version one.

A lot of people that you see in the business world have similar softer personas because that is the ticket to mobility. In addition to the connection between the softer version of masculinity and blackness, there is the light-skin factor, the phonotypical characteristics close to Whiteness.

Orelus: Do you think the way Black men nowadays behave has something to do with the history of slavery?

Bonilla-Silva: I would never deny the historical impact of slavery. Slavery impacted us, and such an impact will last for generations. But I do want to state that after slavery, other forms of oppression continued the pattern; so if one wants to understand contemporary versions of Black masculinity, one has to understand that after slavery there was a continuation of the violence exercised against Black men in the labor market, in the streets, etc. Therefore, Black men have to perform two jobs: (1) to be obedient in public interactions with Whites or else suffer from indignities and potential death, and (2) as a response to this, to be hyper-masculine at home. So, you see my point?

Orelus: Are you saying that racism has something to do with the way Black men behave in society?

Bonilla-Silva: Absolutely! The whole thing is intrinsically connected. By the way, we are talking about Black people, but what about White males who also have the connection to racism in terms of their performance of masculinity? But the subject is blackness. Whatever we Black men do today is deeply connected to the racial order. I don't want to get theoretical in this component, but we did have patriarchy before slavery was inflicted upon us; so it is not that before slavery we didn't have patriarchal versions of masculinity. What I am saying is that after slavery the way we performed masculinity had changed.

Orelus: Black men are targeted wherever they go because of their skin tone. Obviously we cannot stop living, so what should we do? Should we head back to Africa as Marcus Garvey once proposed, or should we try to integrate in the White world as Martin Luther King once dreamed of?

Bonilla-Silva: It depends on how you define blackness. We could say that most of the world is comprised of people of color. If that is the case, we don't need to go back to Africa; we have places and histories. I am, for example, a Black Puerto Rican, so I have the blackness and then the Latino ethnicity. You took the pessimistic view. I would take the optimistic view. OK, it is true that racism has been with us for 500 years; we saw the transition from slavery to Jim Crow, and from Jim Crow to what I call in my work the *new racism*. So, yes, we still have racism but we are moving forward.

There have been fundamental changes in the racial order. If we have to keep ourselves between being a slave and being a person under Jim Crow, I prefer Jim Crow; between being a person living under Jim Crow and a person enduring the hell we live today, I prefer the hell we live today. The struggle will continue.

The hope is ultimately the elimination of race as a category of domination and oppression and to move toward the transformation of race into culture. Will that happen? I remain optimistic. I do know that I will never stop fighting, and I will never tell folks out there to stop fighting. One can pick a totally pessimistic standpoint and say, "you know what, there is no point in fighting because you never win." I feel that had we done that we would have still been enslaved; so our job is to continue to struggle, continue pushing, pushing, pushing but being fully aware that between now and the final liberation there may be all stages. We need to fight this monster we are enduring today while recognizing that in 50 years that monster will hopefully be somewhat nicer.

Orelus: I wasn't suggesting that we should go back to Africa. That is one of the arguments that has been made in the past.

Bonilla-Silva: I know. I do know why in certain moments in history we as people have advocated for the separation option. We still have it in the nation of Islam. However, although there is a beauty in the argument of basically leaving me the hell alone, we are owed for the injuries caused to us by White supremacy. Therefore, our struggle is to get reparations, whether White folks like it or not. We probably have to impose it on them—to provide reparation for the injuries—past, present, and future. I am not willing to go anywhere, neither to Africa nor to the South like some people in the 1930s suggested to leave the south to Blacks. *NO!* I want my money here; in Michigan, Wisconsin, New Mexico, North Carolina, Texas, anywhere that I am; I want my reparation. I want to push for a society in which we truly become a multicultural nation where race is no longer a factor of domination.

Orelus: How do you understand the role that the interconnection between racism and capitalism plays in oppressing people of color?

Bonilla-Silva: You know very well that we in the Caribbean have Eric Williams who told us way back that capitalism was a racialized capitalism. His work has been followed through by other Black scholars. These scholars argue that capitalism, with some exception, was a racialized system. Therefore, the struggle for liberation against racism would also have to be the struggle for liberation against capitalist oppression. The secret of the future is how to articulate a politics that allows us to put together the racial, class, and gender struggle in one struggle. Will that ever be? I don't have a formula, and I don't believe in formulas; but I believe you need to articulate a politics, and I trust movements to develop a fine print of a program to do so. That is the clue: understanding that the racial order is a class order, and it has been so for 500 years.

Orelus: I do recognize that there is a clear link between racism and capitalism. However, I would say there are countries such as Cuba where supposedly there is a socialist system but Black folks are oppressed. So how would you explain this?

Bonilla-Silva: The racial order in Cuba deserves special attention and needs to be critically analyzed. Before Cuba became what it is today, it was in a racial order. Bringing in socialist leaders in the racial capitalist traditions of the past did not transform the culture and the practices of racism there. Therefore, racism is still part of Cuba. Now do we truly want to see Cuba as a socialist order when in reality there is in power an authoritarian regime with a lot of capitalist components to it? But if you push me, I'll tell you ultimately the struggle will continue, whether it is in a capitalist economy, in a mixed economy, or in an economy that calls itself socialist.

The struggle that I suggested before about race, class, gender cannot be one that is limited to one country because the world has been well interconnected. You cannot have freedom in one corner and none elsewhere; that is the way the world system operates.

Orelus: In the US, we are living in a system that is capitalist and racist. Are you saying that in order to come to voice and set ourselves free, we then need to fight both capitalism and racism at the same time?

Bonilla-Silva: Not only in the US. We'll have to develop solidarity worldwide. Think about the struggle that we are having. We will never be free until we understand that our struggle is the struggle of Mexican workers, it is the struggle of workers everywhere. To put it simply, how can the US free itself from the capitalist racist order when Lou Dobbs every night on CNN is telling American workers, "I am for you, therefore, I hate Mexicans." This will never allow us to develop a politics, a morality of class, race, and of solidarity. You cannot realize class and racial solidarity and unite workers of America without having a clear view of the world system. If you don't, your struggle will be limited and you'll collapse.

If the US is trying to engage in this liberation, in the process and you say, "OK now we workers of the world of America are free but we want to get rid of all the minority workers so that we can have our socialist system," it would never work. The system has to be anticapitalist and antiracist at the global level. I am not being an idealist. I understand that people have to start the struggle where they are, so as American workers we need to start making the demands at home. But it is the job of those engaged in the larger politics to make the connections so as to avoid a nationalistic view, which can impede the global solidarity.

Orelus: Many scholars who are from the so-called Third World, when they talk about racism—I am referring to those who are living in the US—they usually focus on racism taking place in the US but not on racism that is alive and well in their native countries. What is your stance on this issue?

Bonilla-Silva: It's everywhere.

Orelus: You're from Puerto Rico, but in your book *Racists Without Racism*, I didn't see any analysis of racism that has been happening in Puerto Rico. I have friends who are from there, especially Afro–Puerto Ricans. They always talk about racism they experienced when they were living there, but you didn't really talk about that in this book. Was it a conscious choice?

Bonilla-Silva: The data for the book were obviously collected in the US. But I gave a talk on the book in Puerto Rico, and I began and concluded by saying that I learned about color-blind racism not in the US but in Puerto Rico. So I do make a claim that racism is not an American problem; it is not a South African problem; it is a world systemic problem. Puerto Rico is older than the US in terms of the contemporary nation-state. Puerto Rico has a nation state a hundred years longer of racial history. We have been playing the color-blind stuff longer than the US. Now the question becomes: Why don't we talk about race in Puerto Rico, Cuba, Colombia, etc.? It is because of the way that the racial order was structured. We have been playing the color-blind drama longer than the US, which means that our racial order is ultimately more effective in maintaining domination than the American order is.

In my recent work, I claim that the American racial order interestingly is moving to a Latin American–like racial order. If that happens, then racial inequality, White supremacy, will be deeper because it is easier to dominate where you have your domination and keep it in the face of everybody to see. In Puerto Rico we claim that we are all Americans, that we no longer see race; we follow Obama's logic. If we follow the nonsense that we don't see any race in this country, that we are all Americans, then we would be moving into the Latin American–like direction. Down the road we would be like Puerto Ricans, Cubans, or Venezuelans. We don't have racism in this country; the only racism in the world would be South Africa.

So the issue for us in the Americas, in the larger sense of the word America, is: How do we develop a politics of race in places where there is no place to talk about race? That is a hard issue. Those of us who are interested in changing our countries, we have been talking about it. I am working on projects that address the race questions in Puerto Rico; but when I was working on this particular book (*Racism Without Racists*) I was getting my feet into academia just like you. Now I am sort of a free man of color, so I can do whatever I damn please.

This Friday I am bringing this colleague, sociologist Tukufu Zuberi, from the University of Pennsylvania. He and I are now working on projects to make connections, pan-African connections. He has deep connections in several African countries and in Colombia, Venezuela, etc. We are working to generate discussions about racial stratifications in the US and in other places so as to learn about how race is structured in places like Cuba, Colombia, Puerto Rico, etc. Obviously as a Puerto Rican, my ultimate goal (it is sort of a personal goal) is to be able to produce work, as well as a politics that addresses race questions in Puerto Rico. I did not start with this even though all my work with regard to race is always connected to other countries. You, as someone who is from the Caribbean, can see the connection. Since I was in Puerto Rico, I always have the desire to address the race issue. Now I am a free man. It is a matter of, "OK. Now I don't have to be kissing anyone's back; I can do what I want to do," which is ultimately the work and politics about race in Puerto Rico and the larger Caribbean.

Orelus: You know all forms of oppression are related; so if we have to fight against racism, we should also fight against other forms of oppression such as homophobia. We know that in the Caribbean there is a lot of homophobia. What is your political and personal position on this issue?

Bonilla-Silva: I do believe that ultimately that is the task of progressive politicians to fight against all sorts of oppression. If anyone is oppressed, then no one is truly free. With that said, I do want to make an appeal for us to be clear that I will struggle fundamentally for my rights. I am not going to expect White people to liberate me. Women should not be silly enough to expect men to liberate them; gays and lesbians should not be silly enough to expect heterosexuals to liberate them. This means that you first organize with your logical allies, people who are in the same position, suffering from the same oppression, and then from there you expand the coalition.

But I am not in the business of believing—you probably can relate to this, those of us who are of a certain age remember the socialist appeal—don't bring your race concerns, your gender concerns, or your concerns about homophobia because we struggle for class, solidarity, and socialism. Socialism obscures everything, and I will point something out that Cuba (you mentioned earlier the issue of racism) has a huge problem with homophobia as well as with patriarchy.

Therefore, although I am solidarity with everyone who suffers from any form of oppression, I know that my fundamental task is to explore the race–class interaction. From there I would express solidarity with other folks and hopefully they will also express solidarity to our movement. Hopefully, we would then have the larger political movement of human emancipation. It is easy to say I am going to join with everybody, with the handicapped people, with people who have been called obese, and with people who have been called ugly. We can, to use Obama's term, get into cynicism. We can make an argument that everybody in the world is oppressed and we have to fight along with everybody. I feel that sometimes we are in a position where we cannot fight.

Orelus: We cannot expect women or Black people to fight against racism and sexism alone because, as you know, we as men have contributed to maintain the patriarchal system.

Bonilla-Silva: Of course. Again because we've benefited from patriarchy, they (women) need to organize. Their struggle is to organize first with their logical allies—all women. From there they should push us, and the hope is that progressive men like you and I join them in that struggle for liberation from patriarchy and sexism as an ideology and as a practice. It would be silly for them to expect us to lead their movement. Where do you begin? Do you begin organizing men? Or do you begin organizing women? You and I as Black men, do you begin organizing Black people? Or do you begin organizing White people?

The logic of the politics has to be: We organize first with people who are experiencing oppression. From there we make a larger appeal. I am not saying that we are not going to make a larger appeal. Are you saying that politics is also about knowing? The tactics? How do you make the tactics that are connected to a larger goal, to a larger strategy?

Orelus: Throughout your work you have addressed racial issues. How did you get interested in this issue?

Bonilla-Silva: As a Puerto Rican, Black Puerto Rican, I never had the 100 percent consciousness of racial matters because that is what Puerto Rico, Cuba, Mexico, and Brazil give you: A sort of divided identity; no space to talk and think about race. Consequently, you suffer individual indignities, which are translated into examples of individual prejudice but not as systemic racism. I came to the US with the sense that racial matters in Puerto Rico are different from those in the US. I thought that as a Black Puerto Rican I had lesser chances in a number of areas in life. I came to the US as a vulgar Marxist to do class analysis. I then joined movements in Wisconsin dealing with racial matters, and that was sort of the beginning of the transition.

Like many Caribbean folks, it was the contact with the US reality that allowed me to rethink my own history back home and to get serious about racial issues in the US. But I am always sort of going back home and thinking about prejudice in Puerto Rico.

Before I started dealing with race in the US, I started reliving my own history and began to be extremely concerned about understanding the racial and historical past of the country that then led me to change my dissertation work. Initially, my dissertation had nothing to do with race; it was on squatting in Puerto Rico, specifically the political economy of squatters in my country. As soon as I became a professor in Michigan, I had already made a motional, political, and a theoretical move into the race terrain and have been in that situation for the last 15 years.

Orelus: Some orthodox Marxists tend to focus more on the class issue rather than on the race issue. In other words, for them it doesn't matter if you are Black, White, or Brown because we're all oppressed by capitalism. How do you understand such a position?

Bonilla-Silva: I was like that for some time. I believed that racism and sexism are an ideology developed by the bourgeoisie to divide workers. But if you are a Black Marxist and someone calls you *Nigger*, it is hard to make an argument that it is simply ideological. You read and understand that White workers do get better rights in this society than minority workers, and that this is not a mere ideology but a practice. I obviously no longer take that position, but I have to tell you that I did, and that is part of the growth, the intellectual and political growth of many of us. We make our politics and our conscience based on our material life. There are spaces, political and cultural, that you could not have ever thought of. In a country like Puerto Rico even calling someone Black is still an issue; there is no space for that; it is an insult. Therefore, no one wants to be called Black.

In the Dominican Republic, there are a lot of dark-skinned folks, but Dominican folks don't want to call themselves Black. For them being Black is being Haitian. They are like, "I am not Haitian; I am Mulatto; I am Indian; I am White; I am Dominican; I am anything but Black." Again, like many Caribbean folks from the Hispanic Caribbean I have developed a political and cultural outlook drawn fundamentally on my experiences and on my milieu. I can give you hundreds of examples of how race mattered in my own life; but there was no space for developing a clear consciousness about racial politics.

Orelus: In your work you also made the distinction between light-skinned Black and dark-skinned Black. Has the whole issue of light skin vs. dark skin influenced your work?

Bonilla-Silva: In the sociological tradition we do a lot of empirical research that clearly shows that light-skinned Blacks as well as light-skinned Latinos do significantly better in life than dark-skinned ones. There is no mystery of why that is the case. Historically, White folks have exhibited a preference to light-skinned children because the assumption is that if you have light skin it is because you're mixed. Malcolm X talked about the field Negroes and the house Negroes. The house Negroes were usually the product of interracial rape. Historically, the system has rewarded lightness closer to the European look; but those of us who are darker have been penalized. With regard to this issue, I did not develop anything new. We have had that for a long time.

What is new in my work is this argument about the US now moving into a Latin American type of racial order, which I claim is going to be of three different groups: Whites on the top, a middle group that I call the orally White, and a large group at the bottom, a morphous group that I call *the collective Black*. If you look at the entire spectrum of people, it is true that some dark-skinned Black folks do well. But if you look at the entire race of people, and you have the data set including all Blacks or all Latinos from all backgrounds as we have had in the past, you'll find that the best predictor of mobility is among people with light skin, who acquire more mobility than the dark ones. So if you come from a poor family and you are darker, you are less likely to achieve mobility than a lighter version of your folks. Similarly in an upper-class family, the darker ones are less likely to achieve mobility than the lighter ones. People always say, "what about Oprah"? Our sociological response is that the anecdote does not substitute the pattern. With the exception of Michael Jordan, there are plenty of dark-skinned folks who never achieve. So we need to look at the collective life chances of Black people.

7
OBAMA'S FOREIGN POLICY AND ITS IMPLICATIONS FOR HIS LEGACY

As I shall be using the term, "imperialism" means the practice, the theory, and the attitudes of a dominating metropolitan center ruling a distant territory; "colonialism," which is almost always a consequence of imperialism, is the implanting of settlements on distant territory.

(Edward E. Said, *Culture and Imperialism*, 2012, p. 9)

Drawing on the current socioeconomic and political situations of Third World countries, including neocolonized and occupied countries like Palestine, Afghanistan, and Haiti, this chapter examines the effects of Obama's foreign policy on these countries and more. In 1965, Albert Memmi wrote *The Colonizer and the Colonized*. In this classic book, Memmi analyzes the unequal power relations between colonized Africans and European colonizers. Specifically, Memmi analyzes the inhumane conditions of the colonized caused by the exploitative practices of European colonizers and imperialists. During the period when Memmi wrote this book, many African countries—such as Cape Verde, Guinea Bissau, Mozambique, Angola, Zimbabwe, Equatorial Guinea, Mauritius, Botswana, Comoros, Seychelles, Lesotho, and Djibouti—were still under the colonial domination of imperialist powers, such as Great Britain, France and Portugal. The rest of African countries had just become independent.

The liberation of Africa from its European oppressors signified a new era of hope for colonized people worldwide who had been subjugated to colonial rules for centuries. Although internal conflicts resulting from the colonial legacy have ravaged independent African nations and caused the death of millions of innocent people, officially these nations were "free." After colonized African countries gained their independence, one hoped that the colonial era would be over and that a significant shift in the unequal colonial power relations between Western countries and non-Western countries would take place. However, these formerly colonized and occupied countries have been experiencing a renewed form of colonization and occupation disguised with a different mask. This chapter sheds light on these issues principally by examining the current political and socioeconomic situations of neo-colonized and occupied countries including Haiti, Palestine, Iraq, and Afghanistan. This chapter goes on to analyze the effects of Obama's foreign policy on these countries.

Oppression, Suffering, and Resistance in Occupied and Neocolonized Lands

Like many countries that were officially colonized, Haiti, a former French colony, has been experiencing a new form of Western colonization and occupation disguised by neoliberal discourse propaganda (Farmer, 2005; Chomsky, 2002; Goodman, Chomsky, Farmer, Aristide, and Aristide 2004; Orelus, 2010). For example, in *Getting Haiti Right this Time*, Goodman et al. (2004) contend that this form of domination is orchestrated through the imposition of US neoliberal economic policy with the complicity of corrupt Haitian leaders and segments of the Haitian elite. Historically, corrupt Haitian leaders—such as the Duvaliers; the Haitian former general, Henri Namphy; former Haitian presidents, Prosper Avril and Boniface Alexandre; and the current president, Michel Martelly—have opened Haiti's doors to Western corporations for cheap labor. Haiti is not the only formerly colonized country that has been victimized by the neoliberal, neocolonial, and corporate policies of Western imperialist countries, however. Other oppressed nations such as Palestine, Afghanistan, Iraq, and Pakistan have also been suffering under Western neoliberal, neocolonial, and imperialist policies. The poor and the struggling middle class living in these occupied countries have suffered the negative effects of these policies crafted by and imposed on them by Western imperialist powers. Imperialist countries have occupied and neocolonized these nations under the pretext that they want to help them to be economically prosperous, politically stable, democratically run, and civilized. This is all known as propaganda. The horrifying psychological, socioeconomic, and political forms of genocide perpetrated on colonized and occupied nations, like Palestine, Haiti, Afghanistan, Indonesia, and Pakistan, by imperialist and neocolonial powers, like the United States, Great Britain, and France, have been internationally exposed.

However, the unprecedented 2008 US election that led to the presidency of Barack Obama had given Americans, US residents, and people around the globe high hope that president Obama, whose father was Kenyan, would adopt a fair and humane foreign policy toward the aforementioned impoverished, occupied, and colonized nations. Unfortunately, Obama's government has proven to be a continual machine of the US empire. Since Obama came to power, there has been no significant change in US foreign policy vis-à-vis developing countries. People across diverse ideological and political positions have critically questioned Obama's "change and hope" campaign slogan, which is yet to be translated into concrete actions and praxis, even though Obama has only about one year left to complete his second term.

Under Obama's command, the United States continues its imperialist and neoliberal foreign policy. Iraq and Afghanistan are still occupied by US imperial armed forces, and innocent civilians—including children and women—continue to lose their lives, despite a global outcry that has erupted, denouncing the atrocious effects of US imperialism on the poor living in these occupied and colonized lands. US imperialism has extended its reach worldwide under Obama's presidency. The increasingly bestial nature of US imperialism supported by the White supremacist ideology of conquest and domination has made and continues to make Obama extremely popular, although not for good reasons benefiting humanity.

Even though Obama is reaching the end of his second term, his political record, which will shape his legacy, seems to suggest that only the skin color of US presidents has changed since the historic US presidential election in 2008. In other words, although Obama is Black—as socially constructed in the United States—his ideology appears to be as white as his conservative White male predecessors. In other words, Obama's discourse toward oppressed nations is not so different from that of his predecessors. Like the White male presidents who preceded him, Obama often uses an imperial discourse when referring to currently invaded and occupied countries, like Iraq and Afghanistan, where nationalist militants or leaders have been resisting US invasion and occupation of their lands.

Like former presidents Richard Nixon, Ronald Reagan, George W. Bush, and Bill Clinton, Obama has portrayed himself and acted like an imperialist warrior president since the beginning of his term. Ironically, he was awarded a Nobel Peace Prize in 2009. This decision from the Nobel Committee showed a complete disregard for the deep psychological, socioeconomic, educational, and political suffering of colonized and occupied poor people caused by US invasion and occupation prolonged by President Obama. In 2011, Obama authorized a deployment of 21,000 soldiers to be sent to Afghanistan to protect US interests. Like US and British soldiers who had already been in Afghanistan for about a decade, these newly deployed soldiers most likely ended up killing innocent civilians, while many others ran the risk of losing their lives and leaving families behind in deep pain. Though there are indeed terrorists in these occupied and colonized lands who are loyal to al-Qaida and who have killed innocent people, thereby posing a real threat to world peace, one must ask: What are the root causes of these terrorist actions? Nobody was born a terrorist. How and why have these people become terrorists? These questions must not be ignored. They must be brought to the forefront of political debates that revolve around US foreign policy toward the poorer, darker, occupied, and colonized nations alluded to earlier.

Like all oppressed people, what Afghan, Iraqi, and Palestinian people need are peace, food, shelter, employment, health care, and access to quality education, not drone strikes or bombs authorized by Obama's government that cause the death of many, including children and the elderly. They do not need occupation of their land by brutal US armed forces or Israeli armed forces financed and supported by Obama's government. Besides Afghanistan, in 2014 Obama announced that his government planned to send another 300 troops to Iraq, supposedly to strengthen security at the US embassy and protect US citizens and property. These additional troops, if approved, will increase US personnel to approximately 800. This decision seems to be a renewed form of US occupation plan of Iraq, camouflaged and hidden behind Obama's political rhetoric and propaganda of democracy and freedom.

The rhetoric around the protection of US soldiers—who should not have been in Iraq in the first place killing innocent Iraqi people—aims at hiding the main reason that Obama's government and previous US governments wanted to send additional troops in Iraq. Like his predecessors, Obama acted as an opportunistic president, taking advantage of the ethnic crisis between Shias and Sunnis (which the US and British occupation has caused) to send US military personnel and soldiers to protect US economic, geopolitical, and imperial interests there. Abdel Bari Atwan, editor of a Pan-Arab website, states, "the main factor responsible for the current chaos [in Iraq] is the US/Western occupation and the Arab backing for it. Any other claim is misleading and aims to divert attention [away] from this truth" (Atwan, as cited in Chomsky, 2014, p. 1). Along the same lines, Iraq specialist Raed Jarrar notes, "this sectarian strife that is destroying the country . . . clearly began with the US invasion and occupation" (Jarrar, as cited in Chomsky, 2014, p. 1).

With regard to the Israeli and Palestinian conflict, Obama's political speeches and actions about occupied Palestine are not so different from those of former US presidents. Like them, Obama has not taken a stance against Israel's occupation of Palestine and subjugation of Palestinian people. In fact, since he has come to power, Obama has supported the aggressive actions of the Israeli government against innocent civilian Palestinians. His silence on the suffering of the Palestinian people raises some fundamental questions, such as: Is Obama a servant of the US empire, wearing a brown mask, with a friendlier face than his White male predecessors?

US invasion and occupation of various nations, like Iraq and Afghanistan, occurring during the presidency of Obama has led to a common thread of suffering that all occupied and neocolonized nations share: they are all under constant fear, terror, or threat of terror. Many of those living in occupied lands—like Palestine, Iraq, and Afghanistan—have been killed and their resources have been exploited by oppressive Western occupying and colonizing powers like the United States and its protégé, Israel. Yet, President Obama has not, and most likely will not, do anything to stop the suffering of these oppressed nations.

Similar to Iraq and Afghanistan, Haiti—another neocolonized and occupied land—has been under the domination and occupation of US neoliberal economic and foreign policies imposed on the corrupt, puppet Haitian leaders.

In the sections that follow, I analyze Haiti historical past, particularly the Haitian revolution and its aftermath. I go on to analyze the recent catastrophic event that destroyed many parts of the country, the 2010 earthquake, and Obama's government intervention to supposedly help rebuild Haiti.

Haiti's Past Revisited: A Brief Historical Overview

Even though Haiti is the first Black republic that fought for and earned its independence from the French colonizers in 1804, it has remained unknown to many people in the world. The Haitian revolution is rarely mentioned in Western world history textbooks. To paraphrase Michel-Rolph Trouillot, Haiti's glorious historical past has been silenced. Trouillot (1995) writes,

> The silencing of the Haitian Revolution is only a chapter within a narrative of global domination. It is part of the history of the West and it is likely to persist, even in attenuated form, as long as the history of the West is not retold in ways that bring forward the perspective of the world. Unfortunately, we are not even close to such fundamental rewriting of world history, in spite of a few spectacular achievements (p. 107).

Since Haiti became independent, Western countries, such as France and the United States, have isolated it diplomatically while at the same time economically exploiting it. In fact, when the slaves sought support from the US government to fight against the French colonizers, the US government turned them down. This government feared that the Haitian revolution would inspire and incite oppressed Blacks (who were still enslaved in the United States) and other disfranchised groups to revolt against their oppressors and set themselves free. When Haiti became independent in 1804, the United States did not recognize it until 1862. The highly respected American journalist Bill Moyers (2010) states,

> In 1804, the slaves rebelled and after savage fighting defeated three foreign armies to win their independence. They looked to America for support, but America's slave-holding states feared a slave revolt of their own, and America's slave-holding president, Thomas Jefferson, the author of our Declaration of Independence, refused to recognize the new government (p. 1).

Unlike the United States, Latin American countries, and African countries that fought for and gained their independence from their colonizers and occupiers, Haiti was the only country that had to pay its former oppressor, the French colonizers, a sum of 90 million gold francs for its freedom. Starting to pay this huge sum of money in 1825, Haiti did not finish paying it until 1947. In all fairness, Haiti should have been the one demanding economic reparation from France, which exploited its human and material resources. Instead, the French government at the time arrogantly demanded that Haiti pay for its independence. Naomi Klein (2010), a world-acclaimed journalist, states, "When Haitians won their independence from France in 1804, they would have had every right to claim reparations from the powers that had profited from three centuries of stolen labor. France, however, was convinced that it was Haitians who had stolen the property of slave owners by refusing to work for free" (p. 1).

In short, since its independence in 1804, Haiti has been used, abused, isolated, and exploited by Western imperialist powers like the United States, France, and Canada, as well as by internal corrupt Haitian leaders and some Haitians from the upper class.

Haiti: The 2010 Earthquake and the Economic and Political Agenda of the West

After almost 200 years of isolation and exploitation, Haiti has ironically become internationally known due to the earthquake that partly destroyed it. This earthquake caught the attention of many, highlighting

Haiti's long-term state of misery and poverty. During this tragedy, many people, including hosts/hostesses and commentators in the US mainstream media, kept referring to the abject poverty of Haiti. However, they failed to critically analyze why Haiti is so poor, except the host of the alternative TV station, Democracy Now!, Amy Goodman, who invited scholars to discuss underlying historical, political, and socioeconomic factors that have led to Haiti's poverty. Instead, conservative commentators and columnists, like David Brooks and right-wing Americans such as Reverend Pat Robertson, have blamed Haiti for its disastrous socioeconomic and political problems. For example, in commenting about the earthquake that partly destroyed the country, Reverend Pat Robertson (2010) stated,

> Something happened a long time ago in Haiti and people may not want to talk about it. They were under the heel of the French. You know, Napoleon the Third and whatever. And they got together and swore a pact to the Devil. They said, "We will serve you if you get us free with the French." True story. And so the Devil said, "Okay, it's a deal."

Similarly, David Brooks (2010), an op-ed columnist for the *New York Times*, argued,

> Haiti, like most of the world's poorest nations, suffers from a complex web of progress-resistant cultural influences. There is the influence of the voodoo religion, which spreads the message that life is capricious and planning futile. There are high levels of social mistrust. Responsibility is often not internalized. Child-rearing practices often involve neglect in the early years and harsh retribution when kids hit 9 or 10 (p. 2).

While attempting to analyze why Haiti is so poor, Brooks inaccurately and unfairly compared Haiti's colonial history to that of other Caribbean countries like Barbados and the Dominican Republic. He argued that, like Haiti, these two countries experienced dictatorship and colonialism, yet they have been doing well economically and Haiti has not. Countering both Brooks' and Robertson's inaccurate analysis of Haiti's socioeconomic, historical, and political realities, I contend that Haiti has been so poor because the imperialist policy of the United States and

France has destabilized it economically and politically. Haiti's state of poverty should be situated in its historical and political context; Haiti should not be superficially and arbitrarily compared to other nations that have not experienced what it has been going through since its independence in 1804.

Before the United States imposed its neoeconomic liberal policy on Haiti with the complicity of corrupt Haitian presidents, Haitian farmers were able to grow crops and sustain themselves and their families. They did not have to buy imported products like rice, beans, and sugar from the United States because they were able to grow these products in their farms. Nor did they have to move to Port-au-Prince and overcrowd it with the hope of finding employment at US-owned factories implanted there.

The implantation of these factories has led many farmers to move to Port-au-Prince, the capital of Haiti. As a former resident of Haiti, I knew many farmers who stayed in Port-au-Prince after these factories were closed. Determined to continue to survive in that city, many built shacks there and in surrounding cities, causing many infrastructure problems. The Haitian government did not oversee and regulate the construction of overcrowded and poorly built huts, which have posed a threat to the safety of many poor Haitians. This safety problem caught the attention of many observers, especially during the earthquake. Relief workers, both national and international, were not able to help and save Haitians who were trapped under collapsing shacks and apartment buildings because of the infrastructure problem that the country has long faced, particularly in major cities like Port-au-Prince and surrounding cities, such as Cite Soleil.

Because of the infrastructure problems and lack of resources, many Haitians lost their lives during the earthquake. Many of my relatives and friends—who experienced this tragedy and witnessed the struggle of many Haitians who were trying to save the lives of other Haitians—stated that those who were quickly rescued from collapsing buildings, hotels, and houses were mostly foreigners, including Americans and UN employees and soldiers. Many Haitians had to use their bare hands and feet to save other Haitians who were trapped under the debris of houses and apartment buildings. The majority of poor

Haitians who were trapped in these collapsing shacks, houses, and apartment buildings did not receive proper assistance from international rescue workers on time. Consequently, they lost their lives.

Many who "survived" the earthquake died of hunger later because they did not receive aid in a timely manner. Meanwhile, the propaganda to restore the image of the US government—which, for example, neglected the poor, the disabled, and the elderly during Hurricane Katrina—was widely spread through the US mainstream media like CNN, Fox News, MSNBC, NBC, and ABC. The United States was portrayed as Haiti's primary savior, while hundreds of poor Haitians were homeless and dying of hunger. The Haitian major airport, Toussaint Louverture Airport, was controlled and occupied by US soldiers and personnel as if the airport belonged to the United States. US and UN soldiers also occupied other parts of the country, including the destroyed presidential palace. F. William Engdahl (2010) states,

> Now, in the wake of the devastating earthquake of January 12, the United States military has taken control of Haiti's four airports and presently has some 20,000 troops in the country. Journalists and international aid organizations have accused the US military of being more concerned with imposing military control, which it prefers to call *security*, than with bringing urgently needed water, food and medicine from the airport sites to the population (p. 6).

Before the earthquake, Haiti had already been controlled and "diplomatically" occupied by UN special armed forces. Initially, these soldiers were sent to supposedly restore peace and order in Haiti after the former Haitian president, Jean-Bertrand Aristide, was ousted for a second time in 2004. Since Aristide's departure, these soldiers have been occupying the country and terrorizing the poorest of the poor Haitians.

To substantiate what I am arguing about these soldiers, I want to narrate what I recently observed and witnessed. The following narrative is drawn upon my own observation and personal experience as a former resident in the island and the testimony of those who have witnessed and directly experienced mistreatment from these soldiers. In recent trips to Haiti before and after the earthquake took place, I witnessed UN soldiers treating poor Haitians as unwanted citizens in their own land. For example, poor Haitians were prohibited from having access to certain beaches that used to be public. However, UN soldiers were enjoying these tropical beaches with fine Haitian women, who behaved as these soldiers' sexual objects. While poor working Haitians were complaining about a lack of reliable public transportation, the UN soldiers were traveling in expensive trucks.

Moreover, friends and family members shared with me that these soldiers, mostly males, were eating at the most fancy restaurants owned by the Haitian bourgeois. To confirm this, I decided to have dinner at a few of these restaurants. I purposely interacted with many of them to investigate who they were, as they did not look like the ordinary poor Haitians. While eating at these fancy restaurants, I quickly discovered that the customers were mostly UN soldiers from Brazil, Nepal, Guatemala, and El Salvador, and privileged Haitians who refused to speak Creole with me, but instead insisted on speaking French. Ironically, the UN soldiers were neither French nor Americans but soldiers from these countries mentioned. It seems to me that these UN soldiers are replanting the seeds of colonization in Haiti under the name of an organization that was created to reestablish and maintain peace and order in countries destroyed by internal conflict and war.

The presence and deliberate actions of UN soldiers in Haiti are a good indicator that a new form of occupation is taking place on this island. This form of occupation might be difficult for some to understand. However, it is obvious to Haitians, especially those who know the history of French colonization and US occupation of Haiti. This form of "new" occupation, as many Haitians with whom I interacted put it, is taking place in the name of "democracy" and "political stability and prosperity." While it is widely believed that the UN soldiers were sent to this island to protect innocent people from being killed, many people in many communities, particularly in the poor ones, shared with me that these soldiers were killing innocent people whom they suspected were causing terror. In fact, in the words of many poor people who shared with me their testimony, the mere presence of the UN soldiers caused them more terror and fear than the "violent Haitians" whom these soldiers were chasing and killing like animals in their own land.

Haiti in Times of Crisis: Obama's Special Envoys as the Saviors?

A few months after the earthquake occurred, destroying many parts of Haiti, President Barack Obama chose two former US presidents, Bill Clinton and George W. Bush, to supposedly coordinate and facilitate the relief rescue effort aimed to "rebuild" Haiti. Prior to the earthquake, Bill Clinton had already been chosen by the United Nations as a special envoy to Haiti. Such a choice reminds one of the colonial period where the French colonial government sent especial envoys to Santo Domingo to defend its colonial interests there. The appointment of former president Clinton as a special envoy to Haiti is questionable for two major reasons.

First, Haiti has a huge oil reserve comparable to that of Venezuela. Moreover, this impoverished country has other natural resources such as iridium, a precious, rare, and extremely expensive silver-white metallic element that has been used in military industry. Besides South Africa, Haiti is the second known country to possess this metal. A Haitian writer, Georges Michel, stated:

> It has been no secret that deep in the earthy bowels of the two states that share the island of Haiti and the surrounding waters that there are significant, still untapped deposits of oil. One does not know why they are still untapped. Since the early twentieth century, the physical and political map of the island of Haiti, erected in 1908 by Messrs. Alexander Poujol and Henry Thomasset, reported a major oil reservoir in Haiti near the source of the Rio Todo El Mondo, Tributary Right Artibonite River, better known today as the River Thomonde (2004, p. 3).

Therefore, it is not surprising that the United States, France, and Canada have shown great interest in Haiti. These countries have tried to keep Haiti under their control for centuries. After the earthquake, they showed even greater interest in this country and a firmer determination to take control over it, preventing, for example, the Venezuelan government from intervening to help Haitians in dire need. Moreover, because of their vested interest in Haiti, these imperialist countries orchestrated two major coups against the democratically elected Jean-Bertrand Aristide, whom they felt would prevent them from geopolitically and economically controlling the island. Engdahl (2010) stated,

The remarkable geography of Haiti and Cuba and the discovery of world-class oil reserves in the waters off Cuba lend credence to anecdotal accounts of major oil discoveries in several parts of Haitian territory. It also could explain why two Bush Presidents and now special UN Haiti Envoy Bill Clinton have made Haiti such a priority. As well, it could explain why Washington and its NGOs moved so quickly to remove—twice—the democratically elected President Aristide, whose economic program for Haiti included, among other items, proposals for developing Haitian natural resources for the benefit of the Haitian people (p. 4).

The second reason why Bill Clinton and his predecessor George W. Bush should not be trusted is that these two former presidents destroyed Haiti with their neoliberal economic policy. For example, Clinton helped the former ousted Haitian president, Jean Bertrand Aristide, return to power in 1994 provided that Aristide would implement his neoliberal economic policy in Haiti. This neoliberal economic policy entails opening Haiti's door to corporations, like Walt Disney, to exploit poor Haitians in assembly factories. Moyers (2010) states:

> Every president from Ronald Reagan forward has embraced the corporate search for cheap labor. That has meant rewards for Haiti's upper class while ordinary people were pushed further and further into squalor. Haitian contractors producing Mickey Mouse and Pocahontas pajamas for American companies under license with the Walt Disney Company paid their sweat shop workers as little as one dollar a day, while women sewing dresses for K-Mart earned eleven cents an hour. A report by the National Labor Committee found Haitian women who had worked 50 days straight, up to 70 hours a week, without a day off (p. 2).

Apparently, former president Jean Bertrand Aristide did not follow Clinton's neoliberal economic order. Instead, he continued to show firm opposition to unfair US foreign policy toward Haiti. Consequently, Aristide was once more overthrown in 2004—a coup orchestrated by former US president George W. Bush government with the complicity of some corrupt Haitian soldiers and members of the Haitian upper class. Before Aristide was ousted, George W. Bush blocked all foreign aid to Haiti, exacerbating the poor socioeconomic conditions of Haitians (Goodman et al. 2004).

It is disheartening that Barack Obama chose these two neoliberal American presidents to help "rebuild" Haiti. One must ask: (1) When was the last time these two men showed compassion for Haiti? (2) Where was Clinton when poor Haitians, fleeing oppression in Haiti, attempted to enter the United States in 1991 but were forcibly returned to Haiti? Why didn't Clinton help them stay in the United States like he allowed the Cuban refugees to do so? (3) When was the last time both former presidents Bill Clinton and George W. Bush cared for Haitians and other poor Blacks? (4) Where was President Clinton when millions of Ugandans were murdered in 1994 during the genocide? Why did not he intervene to save lives? (5) Likewise, why did not George W. Bush intervene on time to save the lives of many poor Blacks when Hurricane Katrina destroyed New Orleans? (6) Is these two presidents' "compassion" for poor Haitians an act of White man redemption? Or is it merely a political move to repair their legacy as imperialist, warrior presidents while at the same time making sure that the US interests are protected in this island, which they impoverished with their foreign policy when they were in office? It seems that President Barack Obama, consciously or not, gave these former presidents, especially George W. Bush, a chance to save face. As the entire world knows, George Bush's decision to invade Iraq and Afghanistan has destabilized these two countries and caused the death of millions of innocent people and soldiers, including American soldiers.

A year after the earthquake, Obama's government tried to block former Haitian President Jean Bertrand Aristide from returning to Haiti after having lived in exile for seven years in South Africa, from 2004 to 2011. It was reported in the media, specifically by *Democracy Now!*, that Obama's government pressed the South African president, Jacob Zuma, to keep President Aristide in South Africa under the pretext that the former ousted populist president, with the support of his massive number of loyal followers, would disturb the 2011 election leading to the presidency of Michel Martelly, a US-chosen president (see Goodman, 2011).

A former popular musician with very limited academic formation and training—he only has a high-school diploma—and who apparently lacks critical political consciousness, Martelly was Obama's safest choice and much-preferred candidate during the last presidential election in Haiti. According to public opinion, supported by the revelation of WikiLeaks (see Goodman, 2011), President Martelly was put in power thanks to the strong support of Obama's government and a segment of the Haitian elite.

A conservative candidate with a neoliberal economic and political agenda, Martelly did not (and still does not) seem to represent a threat to US corporate and imperialist interests. Nor does he represent a menace to the capitalist interests of the Haitian elite, mainly composed of Mulattos and the Haitian Black bourgeoisie; many of whom endorsed Martelly's candidacy and worked tirelessly to put him in power for their own economic and political interests. The infiltration and influence of the CIA in Haiti's political affairs combined with the complicity of the Haitian elite have been historically determining factors leading to the emergence of puppet political figures, like President Michel Martelly. *Needless to say*, US influence, manipulation, and control of the Haitian political and economic system have been partially responsible for the long agonizing socioeconomic and political situations of Haiti. These imperialist practices continue to take place while Obama preaches to other nations about democracy and freedom.

As a case in point, while President Obama tried tirelessly to block former President Aristide from returning to his native land, the former brutal Haitian dictator, Jean-Claude Duvalier, easily returned to Haiti almost three decades in exile. Obama's government made no attempt to stop Duvalier from returning to Haiti, even though he and his father, François Duvalier, are internationally known as monstrous dictators who committed horrendous crimes against thousands of Haitians for nearly 40 years. The US government supported both Jean-Claude Duvalier and his father for decades until the former was toppled down by the Haitian masses with the support of the Haitian middle class in 1986. It can therefore be stated that Jean-Claude Duvalier was given the green light to enter the county because he did not and still does not represent any threat to US geopolitical and economic interests in Haiti. This biased, double-standard type of foreign policy implemented by Obama's government clearly shows that President Obama is essentially a loyal servant of the US empire, like his White male predecessors were and continue to be.

Déjà Vu: US-Disguised Brand of the Same Hypocritical and Imperialist Strategy

Asking former George W. Bush and Bill Clinton to coordinate a relief effort supposedly aimed at rebuilding Haiti after the 2010 earthquake was merely a political facade. Prior to this, a similar political facade took place when the tsunami hit Indonesia. Former presidents Bill Clinton and George H. W. Bush were chosen by George W. Bush as special envoys to Indonesia to "save" Indonesian people. How ironic was such a decision? Historically, the US government is well known for having supporting oppressive governments in Indonesia that defended US interests. For instance, the Nixon government bombarded this country while in power under the pretext the United States was fighting against communists (Chomsky and Herman, 1979). The hidden agenda behind the US terrorist actions was to destabilize the country so the US government could put in power the Indonesian dictator Suharto, who served US corporate interests for more than a decade (Chomsky and Herman, 1979). Former President George W. Bush orchestrated a similar plot in Haiti. They overthrew the democratically elected president, Jean Bertrand Aristide, and helped put in power puppet provisional prime ministers and provisional presidents, such as Boniface Alexandre, who posed no threat to US interests.

As noted earlier, Haiti may not be officially colonized and occupied but it has been experiencing a new form of colonization and occupation through Western neoliberal economic and foreign policies. However, despite this renewed form of occupation, many people, including Americans, had hoped that something positive would emerge from the earthquake, that is, Western powers would help Haiti stand on its feet. This sense of optimism might have resulted from a forum about Haiti that took place in Canada approximately two weeks after the earthquake occurred. At this forum, the Canadian government announced a 10-year plan to rebuild Haiti. Similarly, the former French president, Nicolas Sarkozy, while visiting Haiti on February 17, 2010, stated that he had a plan to rebuild Haiti and hoped that the Haitian government would agree with it. One must ask, however: At what cost? Further, what was the political agenda behind this plan? Would this have been an act of real compassion and genuine desire from the international community to help another nation stand on its own feet and become financially independent and prosperous? Or was it a political strategy of Western empires like the United States, France, and Canada to open Haiti's doors wide to Western factories like garment factories where many poor Haitians have been exploited? Klein (2010) intelligently captures this eminent danger when she states:

> This history needs to be confronted now, because it threatens to repeat itself. Haiti's creditors are already using the desperate need for earthquake aid to push for a fivefold increase in garment-sector production, some of the most exploitative jobs in the country. Haitians have no status in these talks, because they are regarded as passive recipients of aid, not full and dignified participants in a process of redress and restitution (p. 1).

In short, was the agenda behind this reconstruction plan aimed to reoccupy Haiti? Approximately five years after the earthquake, the empty rhetoric about the reconstruction of this county is still circulating in Western media. It is hoped that Haiti would not have to borrow money to rebuild from the United States, France, and Canada with an exorbitant interest rate. These countries owe Haiti a lot for having exploited it for centuries. As Klein (2010) goes on to say, "A reckoning with the debts the world owes to Haiti would radically change this poisonous dynamic. This is where the real road to repair begins: by recognizing the right of Haitians to reparations" (p. 1).

General Conclusion About Obama's Presidency and Legacy

As noted in this chapter and in the previous ones, Obama was promoted and supported by the White establishment, particularly the White mainstream liberal media and the corporate world. With this support, combined with his rhetoric of hope and "change you can believe in," Obama managed to convince the American public, which contributed to his political victory both in 2008 and 2012. Obama's first political victory in 2008 symbolically represented a renewed hope for many Americans, particularly the youth, after eight years of political, economic, and diplomatic disaster during the George W. Bush presidency. Obama's victory sparked spontaneous enthusiastic celebration worldwide, particularly in Africa and the Caribbean, where there is a great concentration of Blacks. As the first elected African American president, Obama's victory gave hope to people around the globe, as his victory seemed to signal a new era in American politics. However, it did not take the general American population and the rest of the world long to realize that nothing substantive was changing or would be changing in the American socioeconomic and political system with Obama's presidency. As his political actions illuminate, in many ways Obama continued the US imperialist, colonial, capitalist, and corporate agenda here and abroad.

His inspiring message of hope turned out to be a deep deception for many of his supporters (including myself), who have been disappointed with both his domestic and foreign policies. One needs to transcend one's uncritical racial affinity and blind loyalty to Obama in an effort to expose the negative effects of his policies on people, including spying on individuals, deporting a massive number of undocumented immigrants, and ordering the murder of "terrorists" that led to the killings of innocent children, elderly, and pregnant women in countries such as Afghanistan and Iraq. Obama's controversial domestic and foreign policies will shape his legacy as president, and such a legacy most likely will not be what his supporters expected from the inspiring presidential candidate who promised that real change would take place in Washington under his command as president.

Elected officials, namely future US presidents who will take over the White House after Obama, ought to work across racial, ideological, and political lines to co-create a path toward racial, socioeconomic, and gender justice for all, certainly not with lofty rhetoric but through concrete actions. As a biracial president, Obama's political victory represented hope for possible racial harmony between White and non-Whites. Had Obama attempted to challenge the White supremacist system and succeeded, he would have inspired many people across the color line to challenge this system. Obama made many promises while running for president and during his presidency. He promised that he would close the Guantanamo Bay prison, which is essentially a death camp. This camp is still open, and prisoners continue to be tortured within. He also promised that he would end the Iraq War. Instead, he has escalated that war by sending more troops.

Finally, his promise to help middle-class families prosper, let alone the poor—whom he rarely referred to in his political discourse—has not been fulfilled. Both poor working-class people and the so-called middle class have been facing economic terrorism from corporations, including corporate banks, which Obama bailed out. These banks have maximized their profits at the expense of poor, vulnerable people. Most of Obama's political promises and proposed plans have been proven futile and misleading, as they were not translated into concrete actions.

REFERENCES

Acuna, R. (2014). *Occupied America: A history of Chicanos* (eighth edition). Upper Saddle River, NJ: Pearson.

Alexander, M. (2010). *The new Jim Crow: Mass incarceration in the age of color-blindness*. New York: New Press.

Anyon, J. (1997). *Ghetto schooling: A political economy of urban educational reform*. New York: Teachers College Press.

Anyon, J. (2005). *Radical possibilities: Public policy, urban education, and a new social movement*. New York: Routledge.

Apple, M. (2000). *Official knowledge: Democratic education in a conservative age*. New York: Routledge.

Apple, M. (2001). *Educating the "right" way: Markets, standards, God, and inequality*. New York: Routledge Falmer.

Apple, M. (2003). *The state and the politics of knowledge*. New York: Routledge Falmer.

Asante, M. (2011). *As I run toward Africa: A memoir*. Denver: Colorado Paradigm.

Assange, J. (2012, November 8). Reelected Obama a "wolf in sheep's clothing." *RT*. Retrieved from http://rt.com/news/wikileaks-assange-obama-wolf-256/.

Austin, F. (2009, April 22). Among college-educated, African Americans hardest hit by unemployment. *Economic Policy Institute*.

Baron, H. (1982). The demand for black labor: Historical notes on the political economy of racism. *Radical America, 5*(2), 1–46.

Bell, D. (1976). Serving two masters: Integration ideals and client interests in schools desegregation litigation. *Yale Law Journal, 85*(4), 470–516.

Bell, D. (1980). *Brown v. Board of Education* and the interest-convergence dilemma. *Harvard Law Review, 93*(3), 518–533.

Bell, D. (1992). *Faces at the bottom of the well: The permanence of racism*. New York: Basic Books.

Bell, D. (2004). *Silent covenants: Brown v. board of education and the unfulfilled hopes for racial reform*. New York: Oxford University Press.

Benjamin, M. (2013). *Drone warfare: Killing by remote control*. New York: Verso.

Berkowitz, B. (2006, January 28). 14 million in federal-based money goes to Pat Robertson. *Media Transparency*.

Bonilla-Silva, E. (2001). *White supremacy and racism in the post–civil rights era*. Boulder, CO: Rienner.

Bonilla-Silva, E. (2003). *Racism without racists: Color-blind racism and the persistence of racial inequality in the United States*. Lanham, MD: Rowman & Littlefield Publishers.

Bonilla-Silva, E. (2010). *Anything but racism: How social scientists limit the significance of race*. New York: Routledge.

Bonilla-Silva, E. (2011). Beyond Obama's historical symbolism: The heavy weight of being Black/Brown in a racist society: A Conversation with Eduardo Bonilla-Silva. In P. Orelus (Ed.), *Rethinking race, class, language, and gender: A conversation with Noam Chomsky and other leading scholars* (pp. 147–160). Lanham, MD: Rowman & Littlefield.

Bourdieu, P. (1990). *The logic of practice* (R. Nice, Trans). Stanford, CA: Stanford University Press.

Brooks, D. (2010, January 15). The underlying tragedy. *New York Times*. Retrieved from http://www.nytimes.com/2010/01/15/opinion/15brooks.html

Brown, M. K., Carnoy, M., Currie, E., Duster, T., Oppenheimer, D. B., Schultz, M., & Wellman, D. (2003). *Whitewashing race: The myth of a colorblind society*. Berkeley: University of California Press.

Cabral, A. (1973). *Return to the source: Selected speeches by Amilcar Cabral*. New York: Monthly Press Review.

Callinicos, A. (1993). *Race and class*. London: Bookmark.

Carr, P., & Portfilio, B. (2011). *The phenomenon of Obama and the agenda for education: Can hope audaciously trump neoliberalism?* Charlotte, NC: Information Age.

Cesaire, A. (2000). *Discourse on colonialism*. New York: Monthly Review Press.

Childs, C.E. (2005). *Navigating Interracial Borders: black-white couples and their social worlds*. New Jersey: Rutgers University Press.

Chomsky, N. (2002). *Understanding power: The indispensable Chomsky*. New York: New Press.

Chomsky, N. (2004). *Hegemony or survival: America's quest for global dominance*. New York: Holt Paperbacks.

Chomsky, A. (2007). *They take our jobs: And 20 other myths about immigration*. Boston, MA: Beacon Press.

Chomsky, A. (2014). *Undocumented: How immigration became illegal*. Boston, MA: Beacon Press.

Chomsky, N. (2014, July 7). The sledgehammer worldview. *Truthout*. Retrieved from http://truth-out.org/opinion/item/24796-noam-chomsky-the-sledge hammer-worldview

Chomsky, N., & Herman, E. (1979). *The Washington connection and Third World fascism*. Boston, MA: South End Press.

Clarke, R. (2014). *Sting of the drone*. New York: Thomas Dunne Books.

Cole, M. (2009). *Marxism and educational theory: Origins and issues*. New York: Routledge.

Darder, A. (2012). *Culture and power in the classroom: Educational foundations for the schooling of bicultural students*. Boulder, CO: Paradigm.

De Witte, L. (2002). *The assassination of Lumumba*. New York: Verso

Dyson, E. M. (2004). *The Michael Eric Dyson reader*. New York: Basic Civitas Books.

Early, G., & Kennedy, R. (Eds.). (2010). *Best African American essays*. New York: One World Books.

Engdahl, F. W. (2010, January 30). The fateful geological prize called Haiti. *GlobalResearch*. Retrieved from http://www.globalresearch.ca/index.php?context=va&aid=17287

Fanon, F. (1963). *The wretched of the earth*. New York: Grove Press.

Fanon, F. (1967). *Black skin White masks*. New York: Grove Press.

Farmer, P. (2005). *The uses of Haiti*. Monroe, ME: Common Courage Press.

Firmin, A. (2002). *The equality of human races* (A. Firmin, Trans.): *Positivist anthropology*. Chicago: University of Illinois Press. (Original work published 1885)

Foucault, M. (1980). Two lectures. In C. Gordon (Ed.), *Powerknowledge: Selected interviews & other writings*. New York: Pantheon Books.

Fredrickson, G. (2002). *Racism: A short history*. Princeton, NJ: Princeton University Press.

Freire, P. (1970). *Pedagogy of the oppressed*. New York: Continuum.

Galston, W. A. (2010). President Barack Obama's first two years: Policy accomplishments, political difficulties. *Governance Studies at Brookings*, 1–12. Retrieved from http://www.brookings.edu/~/media/research/files/papers/2010/11/04obamagalston/1104_obama_galston.pdf

Gerard, E., & Kuklick, B. (2015). *Death in the Congo: Murdering Patrice Lumumba*. Cambridge, MA: Harvard University Press.

Giroux, H. (2008, November 16). Obama and the promise of education. *Truthout*. Retrieved from http://www.truth-out.org

Giroux, H. (2010). *Politics after hope: Obama and the crisis of youth, race and democracy*. Denver, CO: Paradigm.

Giroux, H., & Saltman, K. (2008, December 17). Obama's Betrayal of Public Education? Arne Duncan and the Corporate Model of Schooling. *Truthout*. Retrieved from http://www.truth-out.org

Godwin, P. (2011). *The Fear: Robert Mugabe and the martyrdom of Zimbabwe*. New York: Little, Brown.

Gonzales, A. (2013). *Reform without justice: Latino migrant politics and the homeland security state.* New York: Oxford University Press.

Goodman, A. (2011, March 17). 7 years after ouster in U.S.-backed coup, former Haitian president Aristide prepares to return home. *Democracy Now!* Retrieved from http://www.democracynow.org/2011/3/17/7_years_after_ouster_in_us

Goodman, A., Chomsky, N., Farmer, P., Aristide, J. B., & Aristide, M. (2004). *Getting Haiti right this time: The U.S. and the coup.* Monroe, ME: Common Courage Press.

Greenwald, G. (2014). *No place to hide: Edward Snowden, the NSA, and the U.S. surveillance state.* New York: Metropolitan Books.

Harsh, E. (2014). *Thomas Sankara: An African revolutionary.* Columbus: Ohio University Press.

Hill, D. (2001, September). *The Third Way in Britain: New Labour's neo-liberal education policy.* Paper presented at the Conference Marx 111, Paris, Université de Sorbonne/ Nanterre, Paris. Retrieved from www.ieps.org.uk

Hill, D. (2002). Global capital, neo-liberalism and the growth of educational inequality. *School Field: International Journal of Theory and Research in Education, 13*(1&2), 81–107.

Hill, D. (2004) Books, banks and bullets: Controlling our minds—the global project of Imperialistic and militaristic neo-liberalism and its effect on education policy. *Policy Futures in Education, 2, 3&4* (Theme: Marxist Futures in Education). Retrieved from http://www.wwwords.co.uk/pfie/content/pdfs/2/issue2_3.asp

Hinojosa, M. (2011, October 18). Lost in detention. *Frontline.* Retrieved from http://www.pbs.org/frontline/lost-in-detention

Jensen, B. (2004). *The heart of whiteness: Confronting race, racism, and white privilege.* San Francisco, CA: City Light Books.

Jordan, W. (1974). *The White man's burden: Historical origins of racism in the United States.* London: Oxford University Press.

Kelley, R. (1994). *Race rebels: Culture, politics, and the black working class.* New York: Free Press.

Kincheloe, J., & Semali, L. (1999). *What is indigenous knowledge? Voices from the Academy.* New York: Falmer Press.

Klein, N. (2010). Haiti: A creditor, not a debtor. *Nation.* Retrieved from http://www.thenation.com/doc/20100301/Klein

Kozol, J. (1992). *Savage inequalities: Children in America's schools.* St. Helens, OR: Perennial Press.

Kozol, J. (2006). *The shame of the nation: The restoration of apartheid schooling in America.* New York: Broadway. Ladner, J. (1998). *The death of white sociology.* Baltimore, MD: Black Classic Press.

Leonardo, Z. (2011). Unmasking White supremacy and racism: A conversation with Zeus Leonardo. In P. Orelus (Ed.), *Rethinking race, class, language, and gender: A conversation with Noam Chomsky and other leading scholars* (pp. 31–51). Lanham, MD: Rowman & Littlefield.

Lipman, P. (1998). *Race, class, and power in school restructuring*. Albany: State University of New York Press.

Loewen, J. (1995). *Lies my teacher told me: Everything your American textbook got wrong*. New York: New Press.

Logan, J. (2002, October 15). *Separate and unequal: The neighborhood gap for blacks and Hispanics in metropolitan America*. Report by the Lewis Mumford Center for Comparative Urban and Regional Research. Albany: State University of New York.

Malcolm X. (1965). *Malcolm X speaks: Selected speeches and statements*. St. Louis, MO: San Val.

Malott, C. (2013). *Teaching Marx: The socialist challenge*. Charlotte, NC: Information Age.

Marable, M. (2003). *Let nobody turn us around: Voices of resistance, reform, and renewal*. New York: Rowman & Littlefield.

Massey, D., & Denton, N. (1993). *American apartheid: Segregation and the making of the American underclass*. Cambridge, MA: Harvard University Press.

McLaren, P. (2005). *Capitalists and conquerors: A critical pedagogy against empire*. New York: Rowman & Littlefield.

McLaren, P. (2011). Critical pedagogy in stark opposition to Western neoliberalism and the corporatization of schools: A conversation with Peter McLaren. In P. Orelus (Ed.), *Rethinking race, class, language, and gender: A conversation with Noam Chomsky and other leading scholars* (pp. 97–110). Lanham, MD: Rowman & Littlefield.

McLaren, P., & Farahmandpur, R. (2001).The globalization of capitalism and the new imperialism: notes towards a revolutionary critical pedagogy. *Review of Education, Pedagogy and Cultural Studies, 2*(22), 3, 271–315.

Memmi, A. (1965). *The colonizer and the colonized*. Boston, MA: Beacon Press.

Meredith, M. (2007). *Mugabe: Power, plunder, and the struggle for Zimbabwe's future*. New York: PublicAffairs.

Michel, G. (2004). Oil in Haiti. Retrieved from http://www.margueritelaurent. com/pressclips/oil_sites.html#oil_GeorgesMichel

Mills, C. (1997). *The racial contract*. Ithaca, NY: Cornell University Press.

Moyers, B. (2010). Haiti's problems are rooted in its colonial legacy. *Alternet*. Retrieved from http://www.alternet.org/news/145388/bill_moyers:_ haiti%27s_problems_are_rooted_in_its_colonial_legacy

Muhammad, C. (2008). America's new slavery: Black men in prison. *Final Call*. Retrieved on March 20, 2008 from http://www.finalcall.com/artman/ publish/article_4475.shtml

Nicholls, W. (2013). *The DREAMers: How the undocumented youth movement transformed the immigrant rights debate*. Stanford, CA: Stanford University Press.

Nieto, S. (2004). *Affirming diversity: The sociopolitical context of multicultural education*. New York: Longman.

Nieto, S. (2011). Unveiling and fighting against discrimination in schools and society: A conversation with Sonia Nieto. In P. Orelus (Ed.), *Rethinking race, class, language, and gender: A conversation with Noam Chomsky and other leading scholars* (pp. 75–84). Lanham, MD: Rowman & Littlefield.

Nkrumah, K. (1970). *Africa must unite*. New York: International.

Noguera, P. (2011). Confront racial and gender oppressions in schools: A conversation with Pedro Noguera. In P. Orelus (Ed.), *Rethinking race, class, language, and gender: A conversation with Noam Chomsky and other leading scholars* (pp. 161–167). Lanham, MD: Rowman & Littlefield.

Obama, B. (2004). *Dreams from my father: A story of race and inheritance*. New York: Broadway Books.

Obama, B. (2008). Evolve: Obama gay marriage quotes. *Politico*. Retrieved from http://www.politico.com/news/stories/0512/76109_Page2.html#ixzz38rdCL5Nt

Obama, B. (2008, March 18). Race speech. Philadelphia, PA.

Omi, M., & Winant, H. (1994). *Racial formation in the United States: From the 1960's to the 1990's*. New York: Routledge.

Orelus, P. W. (2010). *The agony of masculinity: Race, gender, and education in the "new" age of racism and patriarchy*. New York: Peter Lang.

Orelus, P.W. (2013). *The institutional cost of being a faculty of color: A critical personal reflection*. *Current Issues in Education, 16*(2). Orelus, P. W., & Malott, C. S. (2012). *Radical voices for democratic schooling: Exposing neoliberal inequalities*. New York: Palgrave Macmillan.

Rickford, R. (Ed.). (2011). *Beyond boundaries: The Manning Marable Reader*. Boulder, CO: Paradigm.

Robinson, P. (2010). Haiti had pact to the devil. Retrieved from http://scarlett-journey.net/2010/01/14/pat-robertson-haiti-had-pact-with-the-devil/

Rodney, W. (1972). *How Europe underdeveloped Africa*. Washington, DC: Howard University Press.

Ryan, W. (1976). *Blaming the victim*. New York: Vintage.

Said, E. (2012). *Culture and imperialism*. New York: Vintage.

Scahill, J. (2013, October 29). Obama presidency marred by legacy of drone program. *Mother Jones*. Retrieved from http://www.motherjones.com/politics/2013/10/obama-drone-counterterrorism-war-legacy

Shapiro, B. (2014). *The people vs. Barack Obama: The criminal case against the Obama administration*. New York: Simon & Schuster.

Shierholz, H. (2008). Unemployment rate reaches highest level in over 14 years. *Economic Policy Institute*. Retrieved from http://www.epi.org/publication/lost-decade-poverty-income-trends-continue

Shierholz, H., & Could, E. (2011, September 14). Poverty and income trends continue to paint a bleak picture for working families. *Economic*

Policy Institute. Retrieved from http://www.epi.org/publication/lost-decade-poverty-income-trends-continue

Sleeter, C. (2011). Reexamining social inequality in schools and beyond: A conversation with Christine E. Sleeter. In P. Orelus (Ed.), *Rethinking race, class, language, and gender: A conversation with Noam Chomsky and other leading scholars* (pp. 67–73). Lanham, MD: Rowman & Littlefield.

Smiley, T., & West, C. (2012). *The rich and the rest of us: A poverty manifesto.* New York: Smiley Books.

Stanglin, J. (2008). Obama denounces Wright's comments. *Suite101.* Retrieved from http://www.Suite101.com.

Stanley, C. (2006). *Faculty of color: Teaching in predominantly white colleges and universities.* Bolton, MA: Anker.

Steinberg, S. (2011). Democracy and social justice in a capitalist society: Is this possible? A conversation with Shirley Steinberg. In P. Orelus & S. Malott (Eds.), *Radical voices for democratic schooling: Exposing neoliberal inequalities* (pp. 223–235). New York: Palgrave Macmillan.

Stone, O. (2014, December 24). Oliver Stone tears apart Obama's empire. Breaking the set. Retrieved from http://www.youtube.com/watch?v=R2kpy YWd0eo on July 29.

Tapper, K. (2007). A Biden problem: Foot in mouth. *ABC News.* Retrieved from http://abcnews.go.com/Politics/story?id=2838420.

Tatum, B. D. (2003). *"Why are all the black kids sitting together in the cafeteria?": A psychologist explains the development of racial identity.* New York: Basic Books.

Tatum, B. D. (2007). *Can we talk about race? And other conversations in an era of school resegregation.* Boston, MA: Beacon Press.

Thiong'o, N. (1986). *Decolonizing the mind: The politics of language in African literature.* London: James Currey.

Thompson, K. (2011, May 18). Cornel West's criticism of Obama sparks debate among African Americans. *Washington Post.*

Trouillot, M. R. (1995). *Silencing the past: Power and the production of history.* Boston, MA: Beacon Press.

West, C. (1993). *Race matters.* Cambridge, MA: Beacon Press.

West, C. (1999). *Wounds of the spirit: Black women, violence and resistance.* New York: New York University Press.

Williams, E. (1966). *Capitalism and slavery.* New York: Capricorn Books.

Winant, H. (2001). *The world is a ghetto: Race and education since World War Two.* New York: Basic Books.

Winant, H. (2011). Unpacking racial and socioeconomic marginalizations: A conversation with Howard Winant. In P. Orelus (Ed.), *Rethinking race, class, language, and gender: A conversation with Noam Chomsky and other leading scholars* (pp. 59–65). Lanham, MD: Rowman & Littlefield.

Young, J.C.R. (2001). *Postcolonialism: A historical introduction.* Malden, MA: Blackwell.

Young, R. (2001). The linguistic turn, materialism and race: Toward an aesthetics of crisis. *Callaloo, 24*(1).

Young, S., & Schwartz, M. (2014). Healthy, wealthy, and wise: How corporate power shaped the Affordable Care Act. *New Labour Forum, 23*(2), 30–40. Retrieved from http://www.sagepublications.com

Zeilig, L. (2008). *Patrice Lumumba: Africa's lost leader*. London: Haus.

Zinn, H. (2001). *A people's history of the United States*. New York: HarperCollins.

AFTERWORD

Pygmalion President, Military Commander-in-Chief, Cheerleader for Wall Street, and Head of the Empire: Obama, Hegemony, and the Promise for Hope and Change[1]

Paul R. Carr
Professor, Département des sciences de l'éducation
Université du Québec en Outaouais

Introduction

It is an honor to write this afterword for my colleague and friend, Pierre Orelus, who has written an insightful, far-reaching and highly significant critique of the presidency of the first African American to hold the office in the United States. I would like to start by openly acknowledging, as Pierre has outlined, that Obama cannot be blamed for the unsightly and entrenched racism, and its ever-still-increasing visible and virulent manifestation, during his presidency; rather, he has been a lightning rod for endless attacks that have, collectively, sought to sabotage his two mandates as president. Similarly, Obama cannot be blamed for all of the deleterious, derelict, and misguided pronouncements, initiatives, and actions that have been articulated and undertaken under his reign. Lastly, it is important to acknowledge that Obama, by his very presence, is a spectacular figure, one who understands and engages in theatrical performance within the mainstream mindset—and he is a likable guy, someone who seems to, proverbially speaking, have his "heart in the right place." I don't want this to sound like an obituary, nor an unrepentant onslaught against an individual who, arguably, inspired so much "hope," to use his main argument for being elected the first time. Yet, it is necessary to offer this backdrop because of the level of criticism and dissension that has suffocated his two presidential terms to actually operationalize meaningful "change," the other main plank of his 2008 electoral victory.

When Obama won his first victory in 2008, as Pierre has outlined, there were a number of interpretations as to why: Bush was such an abysmal failure and people wanted out of the endless military drumbeat for war, the Republican ticket was less than inspiring, people wanted "hope" and "change," and so forth. Another explanation might be that in the United States, the candidate who spends the most money during a presidential campaign has always won, for the past hundred years, and Obama spent more than McCain (Carr & Porfilio, 2009). The fact that he raised and spent more than a billion dollars is not an innocent sidebar. What it means is that Obama consecrated untold hours to meeting with rich, self-interested individuals, businesses, and elites; that he was preoccupied with fundraising; that he often went to dinners, golf games, vacations, and private receptions to raise cash (and, subsequently, mortgage his margin to maneuver)—rather than connect with people, issues, and the building of a social movement for "change." Of course, we all understand that mainstream, normative, hegemonic politics is all about making deals, staying in power, and—what is taught in first-year political science courses—the "art of the possible."

The only problem is that Obama spent a full two years leading up to the 2008 presidential election making exceptionally eloquent speeches and arguments about "hope" and "change," and how things would be different, how America—which is only America in the United States but not in any of the other 30-odd countries in the Americas—would reclaim its glory, its rightful place, and be the innately, inherently force of good that it always had been. Obama led the American people—a good number of them—and the world to believe that, with him as president, the United States would be a force of good, not a warmonger, not a human-rights violator, not a destroyer of the environment, not a racist society, not a society based on injustice and hatred but one that was naturally superior, one that embraced the almost incomprehensible notion of "American exceptionalism." Under Obama, everyone was expecting—based on his masterful rhetorical skills and pronouncement—a better, more decent United States (Chomsky, 2013).

When Obama won in 2008, the world celebrated. In Canada, there were numerous parties and gatherings, as there were around the world. In particular, understandably, those of African origin were almost overwhelmed, if not in complete disbelief. Many others of racial minority origin and from marginalized communities were also stultified. Celebrations were everywhere, and the news—which is an entirely different story, given the pull toward superficial, corporate-based and hegemonically centered distractions—was universal in laying out the portrait of the country's first African American president, exaggerating the support, and very expeditiously interpreting the victory as proof that we were now in a postracial society. Question: What percentage of eligible voters voted in 2004 when George W. Bush won his second term in office? 64 percent. Supplementary question: What percentage of eligible voters voted in 2008 when Barack H. Obama won his historic victory? 65 percent (Carr & Porfilio, 2009). Despite claims to the contrary, electoral, representative democracy in the United States is not in good shape, and the one and only majority within the two-party system in that country is the massive block of roughly 35 percent of eligible voters who choose not to vote; neither of the two official parties is able to garner as much support. The point is simply that Obama is part of a system that has been exceptionally harmful, unjust, and disenfranchising to large numbers of people (Carr & Porfilio, 2011). As I noted in the opening paragraph, it would be foolhardy to pin all of the problems we know on his shoulders, and, at the same time, we cannot avoid acknowledging that he is the "leader," the one who represents the very system that has done so much harm, domestically and internationally.

This brings me to the title of this afterword, the rather wordy and unruly listing of several labels, followed by a more cogent subtitle. I cannot take credit for what I believe the genius interpretation of Obama as a *Pygmalion President*, which was developed by my partner Gina Thésée over what she may have believed to be far too many conversations on the topic, which relates to the uncomfortable reality that Obama is incessantly reminding "America" and the "American people" of the natural greatness of "American society," while also suggesting that "change" is required (for example, the continuous and senseless mass killings perpetrated by Americans against Americans on American soil, or the obvious racism, or the rampant poverty). Nevertheless, when given the chance for serious change, as in the case of his much-vaunted dream of a universal health-care plan, serious educational reform, or an end to seemingly senseless military invasions, he seemed or seems to have caved, to put it bluntly, early and quickly. Obama seems to be articulating, almost endlessly, what "America" should be, rather than what it is. His own experience of personal success—academically, financially, politically—despite the obvious problems that many endure, may have colored his belief that in the United States everyone can make it.

The *Military Commander-in-Chief* is an irrefutable feature of being a US president: you have to demonstrate your unavowed support for the military; you have to use it; and you have to expend resources to keep the military industrial complex at the top of all agendas. I must admit that I am personally surprised that Obama has so willingly been such a proponent of droning (much more so than Bush), the maintenance of Guantanamo, the extension of militarization in Afghanistan, the still sputtering and violently turbulent continuation of Iraq, and the invasion in Libya, and that he has shown unwavering support of Israel in spite of all the evidence related to transgressions and over-zealous behavior during the 2014 attacks on Gaza, and so many other incursions. In addition to the support of dictators and the overthrows of people who should have been supported, such as President Zelaya in Honduras, and the almost unbelievable reluctance to denounce former President George W. Bush, who many believe should be brought up on war crimes against humanity, Obama has been a consistent champion for the US military. Ralph Nader's comment in one of his podcasts that the fact that Obama will not subject Bush to such a charge because he is interested in looking forward, not backwards, according to Obama's own words, is nothing short of laughable. Nader wryly stated that if we took that approach with all other criminals, no one would ever be sent to prison because we would only be looking forward, not at their actual crimes. US presidents are bound to capitalism, the two-party system, and protecting the presidency—and, I suppose, the stakes would be too high for Obama to consider taking such a bold position of actually enforcing international law against war criminals.

Cheerleader for Wall Street could not have been clearer in the wake of the 2008 stock market crash when millions of Americans lost their homes and their prospects of a decent future. The banks were bailed out but not the poor, who became poorer; and the military continued to be underwritten, often with the poor being given no option but to join the army, something the wealthy would never consider. As bankers prospered—and showered themselves with bonuses and perks—many at the bottom, the majority, struggled to make ends meet. Social inequalities are getting more obvious, entrenched and deepened, and the trend during the Obama presidency is in the same direction, notwithstanding numerous speeches about the commitment to the "middle class," which would probably be the working class in most countries around the world. Obama has maintained the tradition to not discuss social classes, and, as Pierre has brilliantly outlined, his commitment to tackling racism (at least formally, frontally, and in a vigorously public way) has been less than noteworthy, according to many African American analysts, including Cornel West, Cynthia McKinney, and the Black Agenda Report.

Head of the Empire is a reference to the sad reality that Obama is not simply a good guy working for good people; he also represents some of the worst and most unsavory aspects of the Empire, undertaking secret, nefarious, and antidemocratic operations at home and abroad. Obama has not dismantled the almost unimaginable and unconscionable network of some 900 US military bases in more than 100 countries. The Empire is not about saving the environment, taking people out of poverty, ending militarization, and leveling the playing field so that the top one-tenth of 1 percent of the population are not given unlimited control over the lives of everyone else. Ultimately, we are entangled in a debate about democracy, and—quite fairly, I believe—Obama can and should be judged on how he has contributed to making the United States more democratic (Chomsky, 2013). In sum, the president of the United States wears a number of hats, and the rhetoric must be juxtaposed with the reality, alongside the real, concrete actions that can be documented, as Pierre has outlined throughout the book.

In the following sections, I elaborate on some of the contextual issues, policy domains, and related concerns with Obama's presidency. Acknowledging that Pierre has addressed some of the issues, I do believe that the additional critique and analysis here is helpful in rounding out the portrait of Obama's legacy.

Inauguration for a Two-Term President

Barack Obama was first elected into office on November 4, 2008, and was reelected in late 2012. During Obama's 2013 inauguration speech, he announced similar promises to those he made four years previously. Upon beginning his first presidential campaign, Obama spoke of "turning the page on history," and "taking foreign policy in a different direction." In 2013, he announced that "a decade of war is now ending," and "we the people, still believe that enduring security and lasting peace do not require perpetual war" (Scahill, 2013). Nevertheless, despite such promising statements, concrete past and current evidence suggests differently. The media coverage that took place during the second inauguration of Obama's presidency focused on either how the First Lady, Michelle Obama, wore her hair with bangs, or what the many celebrities in attendance were wearing, and/or if Beyoncé Knowles was going to lip-sync the national anthem (Scahill, 2013). Issues regarding the war in Afghanistan and Iraq, or racism and discrimination in the United States, among many other critical topics, remained silent and neglected.

On the day that Obama was sworn into his second term of presidency, a drone strike was orchestrated and launched by the Obama administration in Yemen (Scahill, 2013). On that day, his counterterrorism team was finalizing the task of systematizing the US's "kill list" and developing rules for how and when citizens could be targeted and killed (Scahill, 2013). In the year leading up to Obama's second inauguration, hundreds, if not thousands, of people (including children) had been killed by drone warfare.

Should Obama have been more perceptive of the ways of the US political system, was he simply just naïve, or did he understand that being an agent of change would carry with it enormous costs, such as potentially not being reelected? But is staying in office more important than *doing something* while in office, especially since it is clear that the "system" is not amenable to progressive change? This raises the question of why Obama spent so much energy saying that he would change the "system" when, in reality, he has been a strong proponent of it, as evidenced by his full, unremitting embrace of the two-party system, fundraising, wedge politics, militarization, support for Wall Street, etc..

Obama's Changing Positions on Universal Health Care

Has health care in the United States ever been equal and accessible for all citizens? Although it has been argued that the health care system in place prior to the Obama administration was highly inefficient—at least 46 million lacked health insurance and 45,000 people died each year as a result (Young & Schwartz, 2014)—a legitimate question of the effectiveness of the current system needs to be asked.

During Barack Obama's first term of presidency, he implemented the 2010 *Patient Protection and Affordable Care Act* (PPAC), which is more commonly known as "Obamacare" (Young & Schwartz, 2014); at one point after its adoption, one of the late-night television comedy hosts stopped people in the street to ask them what they preferred—the PPAC or Obamacare, and, not surprisingly, the proverbial "man in the street" was extremely critical of Obamacare and preferred the PPAC, unable to discern that they were one and the same. This change in health care constituted one of the many acts in which the current American government, and Obama, have embraced and favored the class interests of the corporate elite over that of average-income families (Young & Schwartz, 2014). The insurance companies still rule the roost, still command huge profits, still charge premiums, and still can limit access, notwithstanding the fact that certain improvements have been made but are far from what all other "developed" societies offer to their citizens.

One of the most shocking imperatives of Obama's health care reform is the "individual mandate," which requires every individual to purchase insurance from private companies: failure to do so results in the obligation for citizens to pay a fine (Young & Schwartz, 2014). Most Americans wished to see a universal health care system, something Obama was unwilling to fight for, in the end, against corporate interests. Miller (2012) has argued that the PPAC is too costly to finance, too difficult to administer, too burdensome on health-care professionals, and too disruptive to preexisting health-care models. In addition to the critique from the left that healthcare is still left in private hands, the right-wing perspective, which has been unrepentant, argues that Obamacare has potentially limited future economic growth, distorted health-care delivery, exacerbated entitlement spending, and erased any meaningful appropriate limits on the powers of the federal government (Miller, 2012). The amount of tax subsidy that an individual receives depends upon whether it is obtained through an employer, what options employers have, and the family's tax bracket, among other factors (Miller, 2012). Importantly, the current health-care system in the United States, even with the Obamacare enhancements, is still somewhat arbitrary and, inevitably, unfair, especially in comparison with universal health care in other developed countries.

As a presidential candidate, Obama promised universal health-care coverage, opposed forcing individuals to buy their own insurance, and declared that health care should be a right for every American—noble and bold statements (Maruthappu, Ologunde, & Gunarajasingam, 2013). Unfortunately, such statements do not currently reflect the US health-care system, and upon entering office President Obama violated his campaign promises. The main question is: Does everyone get access to quality health care without having to pay for it? In 2010, there were more than 50 million people in the United States who were uninsured and unable to receive adequate health care or any at all (Maruthappu et al., 2013); many are now insured, but that insurance comes with a filing cabinet of restrictions, limitations, copays and other stipulations. Sadly, despite seductive rhetoric to the contrary before being elected, Obama did not seriously lobby for alternative, effective, and humane reforms, including single-payer, universal, or public health care for all. However, if there is one achievement Obama can point to, despite the flaws, limitations and problems, it is probably his health-care initiative.

Educational Policy

Since Obama's election and reelection, many scholars and citizens in the United States have been increasingly disappointed in relation to education, the area that many believe to be the fundamental underpinning to any and all potential for meaningful and critical social change. Many Americans have witnessed their nation, and their education system, becoming increasingly threatened by private policy makers, who often dismiss critical learning, critical engagement, social justice, and democracy in favor of engaging in singular pursuits of money and power (Batagiannis, 2010; Carr, 2011; Carr & Porfilio, 2009, 2011, 2015). Policy makers in the Obama administration have continued to dismantle public education, insisting upon instantaneous perfection, the push for privatization, high-stakes testing, and standardized curriculum (Batagiannis, 2010; Bracey, 2009; Carr & Porfilio, 2011; Ravitch, 2010). Within the strictest of neoliberal frameworks, Obama promised to reform American education to promote technology and innovation, and provide more choice—read *charter schools*—for those who do not achieve high standards; however, the expansion of charter schools does not uplift public schools, nor address the target of "high standards," and has not recalibrated the formal education toward greater social justice.

Part of this agenda includes severe cuts in necessary funding for K–12 public classrooms, limiting and/or eradicating teachers' pensions, linking teacher performance to high-stakes testing, and blaming educators for school failures (Carr & Porfilio, 2011, 2015). The Obama administration has failed to sensitize the public to conceptualize education as a social good that has the potential to guide students to become critically engaged and socially transformative citizens (Carr & Porfilio, 2011). It is fundamental for education to be at the base of any dynamic, functional, and socially just democratic process (Carr, 2011; Carr & Porfilio, 2011, 2015).

Richard Mora and Mary Christianakis (2011) argue that, for decades, neoliberal agendas and policies have been reshaping democracy and education in the United States. Obama has furthered the initiative of corporately run schools and has favored privatized educational systems over public education. An extension of this trend can be found in the Rhode Island School Board's decision to fire tenured urban school educators, and, ultimately, blame them for inherent examination failures (Carr & Porfilio, 2011). This policy orientation neglects examining root causes and systemic barriers, seeking the more expeditious scapegoating of poor, racialized, and marginalized communities.

In addition to Obama's promotion of charter schools, Mora and Christianakis (2011) argue that by supporting neoliberal initiatives and policies, Obama has clearly intended to advance free-market models of schooling, ultimately commoditizing and privatizing education. During Arne Duncan's tenure as the head of Chicago's schools, before becoming Obama's Secretary of Education, he introduced the program *Renaissance 2010*, which planned to shut down underperforming urban schools and open new charter or militarized schools (Mora & Christianakis, 2011). Forty-four schools failed to meet academic standards and were ultimately shut down—and the state of Illinois experienced the highest increase of private, charter, and militarized schools in the nation.

Free-market models of school reform have been increasingly promoted throughout the almost six years of the Obama administration (up until 2014, at the time of the drafting of this afterword). Examples of some of the sweeping educational reforms across the United States include union busting, excessive standardized testing, teacher blaming, the rollback of community input regarding school decisions, and the implementation of neoliberal educational policies such as *No Child Left Behind* and/or *Race to the Top*. Tina Wagle and Paul Theobald (2011) outline that policies such as standardized testing are problematic, and continue to marginalize underprivileged and underrepresented groups, while, ultimately, supporting the status quo. Supporters of policies such as *No Child Left Behind* seemingly support it for its accountability measures; however, through critical discourse, it can be acknowledged that inequalities of such measures are clearly visible as it does not take into account absenteeism, or the sufficiency or fairness of testing for English-language learners, or social justice (Carr & Porfilio, 2011, 2015; Wagle & Theobald, 2011). The *No Child Left Behind* policy/framework requires an almost perfect proficiency rate in reading and math tests by the year 2014, and failure to do so results in sanctions, including the loss of federal money. How has such an initiative affected students, educators, and educational institutions? Of course, the objective (while noble) was destined to never be achieved, given that many students with special needs would not be able to achieve the supposedly high standards required by the law. Obama has been critical of the law, seeking a more inclusive, participatory and fundamentally engaged approach; yet, fundamental tenets have not been entirely dismantled.

In 2008, Obama stated that he wanted to provide funds for states to implement a broader range of assessments that could evaluate higher-order schools as well as the ability for students to engage with technology, conduct research, engage in scientific investigations, solve problems, and present ideas (Onosko, 2011). This led to one of the biggest educational policy reforms under the Obama administration—the *Race to the Top* program—and $330 million was spent on new assessments designed to ensure that "all" students would gain the necessary skills and knowledge to succeed in college and the workplace (Onosko, 2011). *Race to the Top* was intended to bolster education in numerous states encouraging the expansion of charter schools, in addition to high-stakes testing and test-score driven accountability (Carr & Porfilio, 2011, 2015). The notion of critically engaged teaching and learning opportunities that seek to develop the underpinning of a more robust, thicker democracy is absent from current educational initiatives introduced and led by the Obama administration, ultimately fueling neoliberalism and inequitable power relations (Carr, 2011; Carr & Porfilio, 2011).

Onosko (2011) contends that, under the Obama administration, national common curriculum standards, textbooks, and guidelines for mathematics and language arts homogenize and centralize classroom teaching and learning. In addition, teacher and administration removal, retention, and merit-based pay and/or bonus pay based on student test scores will, inevitably, undermine teacher/student relations, student-centered curriculum, professional and student engagement, and teacher recruitment. All too often, neoliberal policies criticize and vilify educators, ultimately reducing the status of teachers, ensuring that many talented and motivated young people will not become educators, and may even not complete their studies (Onosko, 2011).

The educational policies that have been implemented employ a rhetoric of crisis about a dire economic future, and offer test-score surveillance as the central strategy to supposedly motivate educators to "develop" children in narrow and limited processes for economic and national purposes (Onosko, 2011). Employability is the focus, not building a better, more decent society. Programs such as *Race to the Top* have organized and created competition in schools, and have tied school financing to middle-class norms (Hairston, 2013). Through such measures of testing and standardization, middle-class, and, ultimately, primarily White students and institutions are more likely to succeed compared to other groups that have been systematically excluded from the same educational opportunities (Hairston, 2013); yet, it should be noted, many working-class Whites continue to face systemic and far-reaching challenges. Standardization, competition, and assessment to measure performance continues the hegemony of the status quo and discriminates against children who are less privileged (Hairston, 2013).

Business-driven educational policies and the expansion of charter schools have proven to be extremely seductive results of the chaos being created, and, as a consequence, many believe that the final answer is the complete dismantlement of a meaningful public education system (to which Obama has offered little resistance). It is important to recognize that the encroachment on public goods such as education and health care by private and special interests will only take society further away from the goal of a socially just, and participatory, democracy. In market economics, neoliberal policies and initiatives will increase social inequalities by encouraging unbridled capitalization, which largely leaves minorities, marginalized and underprivileged youth, special-needs students, and English-language learners at a competitive disadvantage. Of course, there are exceptions to the rule, but the strongly entrenched hegemonic focus on materialism and individualism ensures a reproduction of social relations.

What is necessary and needed in modern and progressive societies is a broadly responsive, socially relevant, and pedagogically engaged educational system (Carr, 2011; Carr & Porfilio, 2011). In a participatory and engaged educational system, critical teaching and learning is cultivated, and the realization that knowledge is socially constructed can be advanced and discussed (Carr & Porfilio, 2011). Transformative education requires a conceptual framework of analysis—and the potential for positive, critical, engaging education within school structures and society at large must be considered and planned, as it unlikely to happen otherwise. Thus, the necessity and fluid connection between democracy and education can—and, in my mind, should—be an objective (Carr, 2011; see also the Democracy, Political Literacy and Transformative Education website at http://www.education4democracy.net/ for a cataloguing of what education for democracy might look like). Critical and engaged learning is fundamental in order to combat social inequalities, injustices, racism, economic, and environmental concerns; yet, the Obama reforms in education represent a clear continuation from the Bush era.

Obama and Foreign Policy

Throughout Obama's inaugural speech in 2009, he promised to use technology as a means to harness the sun and wind to fuel America's cars and run its factories and industries (Rohde, 2012). Oddly enough (and surprising to many), technology has enabled Obama to expand the executive branch's ability to wage hi-tech, clandestine war. Under the Obama administration, the CIA has continued many unseemly and unsightly activities, maintaining the same linear approach as preceding presidents (Rohde, 2012). Throughout Obama's presidency, he has approved more targeted killings than any other modern president. Disturbingly, the Obama administration has declined to reveal the details of how it places people on kill lists, conducts surveillance in the United States, and decides whom to detain overseas (Rohde, 2012).

Presidents Bush and Obama have presided over building an increasingly overzealous NSA, step by secret step, into a digital panopticon designed to monitor the communication of every American and foreign leader worldwide (McCoy, 2014). The Snowden, Manley, and WikiLeaks cases are cataclysmic examples. Not only does such surveillance help gain intelligence that is potentially advantageous to US diplomacy, trade relations, and war making, but it also gathers intimate information for leverage to blackmail in sensitive global dealings and negotiations (McCoy, 2014).

It is true to some extent that Obama has cut back modestly on costly armaments and the size of the military; however, he has invested billions of dollars towards a new architecture for global power and information control (McCoy, 2014). If one is to add the $791 billion used to expand the Department of Homeland Security to the $500 billion spent on increasingly paramilitarized versions of global intelligence in the dozen years since the September 11 attack, then Washington has made a $1.2 trillion investment in a new approach for world power, not to mention the trillions of dollars spent on inherent wars (McCoy, 2014). The recently reinvigorated incursion in Iraq is sure to increase military spending without any clear end in sight.

Henry Giroux (2013) raises many important questions with regard to the role of President Obama and the linkage to democracy and education, such as: Can society truly hope for justice and a better world for humanity in a country that has allowed the bombing and killing of an untold number of citizens in numerous countries, spies on its own citizens, and has the highest number of mass incarcerations worldwide, among a number of other compelling issues? How is hope possible when society is so entwined with dismal and senseless killing, cruelty and human rights violations as well as needless wars such as in Afghanistan and Iraq? Is there any hope and/or acceptance in the United States for young protestors, or, rather, is there an infinite tolerance for the crimes of bankers, hedge fund managers, and corporate polluters? How is hope to make a difference in a country in which competition and wealth drive both economics and politics, rather than any notions of compassion and/or respect for the public good? Throughout any critical discourse, self-reflection is key, and the concept of "hope" under the Obama administration raises many important critical concerns and questions, especially in relation to the growing sense of corruption underlying any form of politics in American life (Giroux, 2013).

The United States, the wealthiest country in the world, is ranked 27th out of the 30 most developed countries for child poverty, among a number of other dire and threatening rankings (Giroux, 2013). More than 350,000 Americans with advanced degrees applied for food stamps in 2010, millions of young people are crushed yearly under the burden of student loans, an increasing number of youths are becoming homeless, and more than 50 million Americans are uninsured or underinsured (Giroux, 2013). The new health-care legislation has ameliorated some of the situation in relation to access; however, the cost dilemma is still a reality for many citizens, especially those in the working and middle classes. While political exhaustion and impoverished intellectual visions are fed by the widely popular assumption that there are no alternatives to the present state of affairs, hegemony successfully suffocates the call for necessary change. Yet, many groups are calling for change, outside of the mainstream media's glare—and many of these groups believed that Obama would be their champion, something that has sadly not materialized.

Drone Warfare

Upon taking office in 2008, Obama pledged to end the "war on terror," and to restore respect for the rule of law in relation to America's counterterrorism policies (Boyle, 2013). Rather than fulfilling such promises, Obama has proved to be just as ruthless as his predecessor, who embarked on a reckless venture of what Peter McLaren refers to as "permanent war." One of the most distinctive elements of the Obama administration's approach is the embracing of Unmanned Aerial Vehicles (UAVs), also known as *drones*, which are being used to kill a range of people, including many innocent women and children, in Afghanistan, Pakistan, Yemen, and Somalia as well as in other areas. In Obama's first year of presidency, he launched six times more drone missions than Bush did during his eight years in office (Boyle, 2013). President Obama has waged his war on terror in the shadows, by using drone strikes, special operations, and sophisticated surveillance to undertake a brutal, covert war against real and perceived networks through a host of questionable means (Boyle, 2013).

Regardless of Obama's unfulfilled promises, the United States has yet to engage in a serious analysis of the strategic costs and consequences of its use of drones, both for its own "security" and that of the rest of the world, and most Americans are unaware of the dramatic scale of the drone program operating under the Obama administration (Boyle, 2013). The analysis that is undertaken is about the effectiveness of drones, taking into account the losses for the "bad guys," without asking critical and necessary questions, such as: Does drone warfare assist in easing global tensions? Does it encourage diplomacy? What do America's enemies gain by being subjected to a policy of constant surveillance and attack? How does droning affect the balance of world power? What will be the result when other countries start to use drones against the United States on US soil, just as the United States is using them against many populations on their own soil? What is lost socio-economically by the continuous development of military means such as drones? Or quite simply, why, in 2014, do hundreds of innocent children and citizens around the globe die daily as a result of war, drones, or senseless killing?

Drone strikes are believed to have killed more than 1,500 people in Pakistan and more than 400 in Yemen since Obama took office.[2] In a series of recent interviews, current and former administration officials have outlined what could be described as the "Obama doctrine" regarding the extensive use of force and the so-called clean war in Afghanistan and Iraq (Rohde, 2012). Under the Obama administration, multilateralism, drone strikes, and a supposedly light US military presence in Libya, Pakistan, and Yemen have been embraced.

Obama has contended that drones have rarely caused civilian death and have been operated carefully, precisely, and "surgically" (Rohde, 2012). To what extent and exactly how are drones to be considered *surgical*? Under Obama, drone strikes have become too frequent, too unilateral, and too often associated with the heavy-handed tradition of US hegemonic power. Rohde (2012) further contends that, from the start, the Obama administration has been eager to differentiate its approach in Pakistan and Afghanistan from that of the Bush administration, which was considered too aggressive with the use of combat personnel. Therefore, the Obama administration adopted a unilateral, "get tough" approach that utilizes less manpower but greater technology.

Under Obama, drone warfare has escalated rapidly, from 33 drone strikes in 2008 to 53 in 2009, increasing to 118 in 2010, and exponentially after that (Rohde, 2012). In Pakistan, for example, public anger over the spiraling strikes has grown, and more and more innocent civilians have been killed. In March 2011, a drone strike that killed four alleged Taliban fighters and 38 civilians stimulated debate in congress. Meanwhile, Pakistan's army chief, General Ashfaq's Parvex Kayari, issued an unusual public statement that acknowledged that a group of tribal elders had been "carelessly and callously targeted with complete disregard for human life" (Rohde, 2012). US intelligence officials dismissed the claim, as one official told the associated press that "there

[was] every indication that this was a group of terrorists, not a charity car wash in Pakistan's hinterlands" (Rohde, 2012). As such evidence demonstrates, critics inside and outside of the US government argue that the Obama administration has adopted a de facto "kill, not capture" policy.

After NATO airstrikes mistakenly killed 24 Pakistani soldiers on the Afghanistan/Pakistan border, many demanded an end to all US airstrikes. Instead, the strikes have increased, and Rohde (2012) argues that the ranks of Al-Qaeda have expanded in the Arabian Peninsula from 300 fighters in 2009 to more than 1,000 in 2012, in part because of the aimless killing by drones. The missile strikes that allegedly kill members of Al-Qaeda and its affiliates in Pakistan and Yemen do not strengthen the economy, curb corruption, or improve government services. David Barno, a retired lieutenant general who commanded US forces in Afghanistan from 2003 to 2005, believes that hunting down senior terrorists over and over again is not a long-term solution (Rohde, 2012). In the United States, civil liberties and human rights groups are increasingly concerned with the breadth of powers Obama has claimed as he wages a new kind of war. The Obama administration has claimed the power to carry out extrajudicial executions on the basis of evidence that remains secret—never seen or discussed by the public—further exacerbating anger and suspicion. The question of the compatibility with the US constitution and/or international human rights conventions is a very legitimate one.

For now, keeping drone strikes covert prevents US and international courts from reviewing their constitutionality. If not opposed or stopped, such privilege and authority is going to be used by the next administration, and the next after that, while a silenced debate will only encourage more illicit killing. One cannot imagine the reaction in the United States if such attacks were launched on American citizens on American soil.

Afghanistan War

In September 2011, Obama declared an end to the war in Afghanistan and promised to withdraw US troops. Nevertheless, after years of fighting under the Bush administration, Obama has had to "sell" to the American public the renewed effort in Afghanistan and bordering Pakistan in order to maintain support for his military and economic policy (McCrisken, 2012). Throughout a number of Obama's speeches and announcements, he has drawn heavily on the idea of "sacrifice" to justify the deepening of the commitment to the war, arguing that the costs of the military are necessary in order to keep the United States safe from further threatening attacks (McCrisken, 2012). Obama has argued that American and other sacrifices that are being made in a number of countries are absolutely essential and justified in order to protect the US public at home (McCrisken, 2012). It is sometimes difficult, if not incomprehensible, to believe that bombing innocent civilians will somehow protect American security; rather, it will likely lead to the contrary, more war, violence, instability, and insecurity.

In 2009, when Admiral William McRaven had been promoted to Commander of the US Special Operations Command (SOCOM), he and his special operations forces were operating in more than 100 countries (Scahill, 2013). After four years as Obama's senior counterterrorism advisor, CIA Director John Brennan became known as the "Assassination Czar" for his role in drone strikes and other targeted killing operations (Scahill, 2013). During Obama's second term, Brennan had created a "playbook" for crossing names off the America's initial kill list (Scahill, 2013). In addition, the counterterrorism team had developed what they referred to as the "Disposition Matrix," a database full of information on suspected terrorists and militants that would also provide options for killing or capturing targets. In early 2013, a Department of Justice white paper laid out the "Lawfulness of a Lethal Operation Directed Against a Citizen," which stated, rather incredulously, that the government need not possess specific intelligence indicating that an American citizen is actively engaged in an active terror plot in order to be cleared for targeted killing (Scahill, 2013).

Continued Support for Wall Street

In general, the support for Wall Street or the interests of the "average" American has been staunch and unrepentant. Paul Street (2014), a prolific scholar and writer, documents how Obama has not vigorously supported the *Employee Free Choice Act*, which he discussed during his election campaign and that would have relegalized union organizing. State capitalism has been pushed to a new level under the Obama administration, highlighted by its continuous and eager support for the *ecocidal* practice of hydraulic fracturing/fracking, an extraction of fuels that heavily pollutes and endangers fresh water supplies (Street, 2014).

In the beginning of 2014, the White House orchestrated the latest *National Climate Assessment*, in which Obama openly spoke on behalf of "clean energy" in front of a Walmart Supercenter. The paradox of this situation is that Walmart has a long and notorious record of being an antiunion employer (Street, 2014). In addition, Walmart has played a leading role in the destruction of manufacturing jobs in the United States by operating as a giant sales platform for goods that are produced in China and other cheap-labor zones (Street, 2014). As human suffering increases daily, Obama has shown greater interest in Wall Street, its advisors, and the rich and wealthy, rather than in social services for families, children, and society, in general. Many necessary services have been severely cut back, under- and misplaced-employment is soaring, and many youth of color are disappearing into poverty, despair, prison, and homelessness (Giroux, 2009). Jobs are being created, but many of them are low-end, contractually limited, careerless types of employment that do not alter the balance of power.

Former President George W. Bush and the current Obama administration have somehow managed to spend trillions of taxpayer dollars on neoliberal policies that include initiating a global and domestic empire of Orwellian electronic surveillance, repeated foreign interference, invasion and occupation, drone warfare, secret prisons; and that supported a colossal bailout of Wall Street firms whose managers remain above the law (Street, 2014). In regards to the environmental impact, the Obama administration's meager proposal to reduce the US carbon-dioxide emissions by a mere 17 percent below the 2005 level by 2020 belies any claims that the United States is serious about environmental sustainability (Foster, 2013). In the United States, the addiction to fossil fuels is built into the Obama administration's DNA, and this includes and involves military ventures to secure such resources (Foster, 2013). The Obama administration is not only promoting the maximum extraction/production of fossil fuels in the United States and Canada but it is also actively encouraging other countries—such as China, Poland, the Ukraine, Jordan, Columbia, and Mexico—to develop unconventional methods that will further harm the environment (Foster, 2013). Meanwhile, Washington has used its influence in Iraq to boost its crude oil production (Foster, 2013). Suffice to say, unrestrained militarization is not good for the environment, and bombing countries can only lead to long-term contamination and destruction (Carr, 2011).

Washington remains little more than a conduit for the oil corporations and capitalists, in general, where climate policy is concerned, reflecting what Curtis White has called "capitalism's barbaric heart" (Foster, 2013). More than 50,000 people have pledged to put their bodies on the line to block construction of the Keystone XL pipeline, thereby facing arrest if the Obama administration gives the northern leg of the pipeline extension the green light (Foster, 2013). At the time of the writing of this text a final decision on Keystone had not been taken but many speculate that he will ultimately support it if he is consistent with his muted commitment to the environment, as well as his vision maintaining a focus on using finite fossil fuels to underwrite the US economy. There is not enough space here to discuss the environmental practices of the current Canadian government but, suffice to say, they are as distressing and debilitating, essentially embracing tar sands, mineral extraction, and pollution as a convenient backdrop to Big Business profiteering.

Race and Racism

Henry Giroux (2009) argues that Obama won the 2008 election because he was able to mobilize a large number of African Americans, two-thirds of all Latinos, and a large proportion of young people under the age of 30 who voted, while the majority of White Americans voted for the John McCain–Sarah Palin ticket. While *postracial* may mean "less-overt racism," the claim that society has moved into a postracial period in American history is not merely premature but it is an act of willful denial and ignorance (Giroux, 2009).

The myth of postracial America has been undermined by a number of recent events, such as Hurricane Katrina, *Brown vs. Board of Education* (resegregation of American schools), the "clash of civilizations" thesis that promotes the idea of a war against Islam, the backlash facing immigrant workers, and the grotesque prison industrial complex, among other factors (Giroux, 2009). The discourse of the postracial state ignores how political and economic institutions, with their circuits of repression and disposability, and their technologies of punishment, connect and condemn the fate of many impoverished youth of color in the inner cities to persisting structures of racism, thereby retaining a state of inferiority and oppression (Giroux, 2009).

The recent (legal) murder of Trayvon Martin and the New York City anticrime "Stop and Frisk" program illustrate how the United States continues to utilize legal measures that perpetuate the subjugation of black males (Brown, 2013). Data released by the New York major's office show that 87 percent of people who were stopped in 2012 were Black or Latino, while 9 percent were White (Brown, 2013). Stop and Frisk remains in place, regardless of crime data that strongly suggests New York City is not a safer place as a result of this policy, and, importantly, that it is a highly discriminatory and racist practice (Brown, 2013).

There remain spurious links between race and crime in North America. Owen Brown (2013) revisits the work of W.E.B. Dubois' classical analysis of Black Philadelphians to demonstrate that race continues to be consequential in contemporary America, despite the reelection of an African American president. Essentially, the inconvenient truth is that historically the US justice system has ultimately failed African Americans (Brown, 2013). Trayvon Martin and Jordan Davis are two of the latest examples in a long line of young Black males whose lives have been abruptly ended because of the fear and loathing of far too many Whites towards African Americans (Brown, 2013). As a result of society's erroneous ideas regarding race, countless African Americans have been killed—including Emmitt Till, Medgar Evers, Malcom X, Martin Luther King, Jr., Yusef Hawkins, Amadou Diallo, and Sean Bell, to name but a few (Brown, 2013)—and thousands are killed annually.

W.E.B. Dubois anticipated the alternative approach to explaining race and crime, from the perspective of concentrated poverty, economic deprivation, and continuing racial discrimination (Brown, 2013). More than 100 years after Dubois' observations regarding Blacks and crime in

American urban centers, many scholars acknowledge and confirm the ideals and practices of racial bias in law enforcement, and how antidrug policies substantially influence many individuals' life opportunities and experiences (Brown, 2013).

The point here is that if Obama does not wish to have the hard conversations about race when he has the power to do so, who then will have them? It is unrealistic to think that a President Bush or others would be interested in doing so. Race, racialization, and racism are embedded in the fabric of the American State, and to ignore that reality is to further entrench racial injustice in everything that happens within the State, including incarceration, police behavior, judicial processes and decisions, militarization, economics, politics, education, and day-to-day life. One can understand why Obama is motivated to not engage in these debates—but, given his enormously powerful rhetoric about hope and change, how could he not fight for social justice at the most visceral, fundamental level, knowing that many people of color are facing systemic, institutional and deep-seated racial conflicts? If Obama believes that it's all about "business as usual," appeasing power brokers and maintaining a stable capitalist state for investors, then it is almost inconceivable that meaningful change for a large number of racialized peoples could be effected.

Guantanamo Bay Detention Center

Throughout his first term of presidency and now in his second, Obama has failed to follow through on his promise to close Guantanamo Bay, and instead signed a bill that provided $633 million for its ongoing operations in 2013. The sheer amount of resources to keep a small number of individuals imprisoned—without trial!—is nothing short of astounding, not to mention highly questionable, if not illegal. Amy Goodman and Nermeen Shaikh (2013) have reported that, while speaking at a White House news conference, Obama called the indefinite imprisonment of more than 100 people unsustainable but defended the ongoing force feeding of those on a three-month hunger strike to win their freedom. Many detainees' attorneys have pushed for the urgent closure of Guantanamo Bay as well as the immediate release of approximately 86 individuals who have already been cleared for transfer (Goodman & Shaikh, 2013). Nevertheless, such calls remain unanswered, and most Americans have no idea of this debacle; rather, most would probably be disheartened to learn of the senseless waste of funds, if not seduced by the need to protect the United States from, in this case, alleged terrorists.

Adam Hudson (2014) provides an analysis of the 154 men currently remaining at Guantanamo Bay, of which approximately 50 detainees have been designated by the Obama administration for "indefinite detention" (in which detainees are said to be too difficult to prosecute due to inadmissible, insufficient or torture-obtained evidence, and are too dangerous to release). Indefinite detention directly violates international human rights laws; however, Obama has embraced this practice since first stepping into office.

Conclusion

This afterword has provided a robust and critical survey of some of the concerns and problems enveloped in the Obama regime as well as a potential forecast of his legacy. To be sure, Obama has faced an almost unprecedented assault from various sectors of the American people—gun owners, free marketers, freedom lovers, patriots, and a host of others, some from the right-wing tea party and others from progressive elements of the peace, environmental, antiracist, and human rights movements. Obama has been contested from the Right with the seriously comical accusation that he is a communist, a socialist or some other type of radical ideologue hell-bent on turning the United States into a collectivist ensemble of kibbutzes or something worse. The right-wing controlled mainstream media, especially talk radio, have maintained an incessant campaign of misinformation and ludicrous fearmongering about Obama being a Muslim and African by birth despite substantial documentation to the contrary. Question: What kind of lunatic Muslim would go to the same Christian church for more than two decades, get married in a Christian church, baptize his children in the Christian church, immediately go to a Christian church after being installed/inaugurated—twice!—and repeatedly stress his Christian roots and allegiance? The time wasted on Obama being born in Africa is not worthy of any space here. As for the Left, progressives have not had it easy. They have been told such things as: "with support like yours, he can only fail," "why don't you give him a

chance?" "he's better than the others," "to not support him is to undermine minorities." Those on the Left have largely been disappointed, to
not say completely baffled and deceived. From my own humble vantage
point, I can only think that if Obama is a true socialist or communist,
he must be taking a large quantity of hallucinogens on a daily basis to
make it through the policies he has supported.

Being president of the United States is not an easy job, and being a
president wishing for and espousing real, meaningful change is equally
difficult. My own reading of the legacy of US presidents is that the one
who seems to have been most honorable, in and after office, is the one
who has been most maligned as weak, not militarist enough, not true
to the "American" spirit, etc.: Jimmy Carter only lasted for one term
and is not considered to be a strong president, but Ronald Reagan is
often invoked, even by Obama, as a true "American," one who made the
United States a much better place. Some recent polls have indicated that
George W. Bush is more popular than Obama. Many "Americans" are
outraged by the health-care reforms, wishing to repeal them, and many
on the Left believe that they have not gone far enough. In all fairness, the
reforms are better than the previous system, but they still maintain the
same inequities, power imbalances, and propensity toward profit rather
than healing. Thousands of Americans continue to be killed annually in
the United States by handguns, violence toward women continues, res-
idential segregation continues, massive incarceration of African American youth continues, and the US quest for militarization and Empire
continues unabated. As for the legacy of Obama and his eight years as
president of the United States, at this time in history it doesn't look
good but . . . time will tell. The beginning of a critical and far-reaching
analysis of that legacy has been wonderfully commenced and outlined in
this book, and I congratulate Pierre Orelus for his prolific and engaged
scholarship, especially in relation to a topic that is complex, problematic,
and fraught with pitfalls, accusations, and complaints.

Notes

1   I gratefully acknowledge the funding and support from Social Sciences and Humanities
    Research of Canada (SSHRC) for my research project, as principal investigator, entitled
    Democracy, Political Literacy and Transformative Education (DPLTE), which facilitated
    the writing of this afterword. I would also like to thank my research assistant, Lauren

Howard, for her assistance. For more information on the DPLTE project, please go to http://www.education4democracy.net.

2　See the work of the London-based Bureau of Investigative Journalism at http://www.thebureauinvestigates.com/category/projects/drones/drones-graphs/.

References

Batagiannis, S. C. (2010). Obama's educational policy: Disposition of authenticity or the politics of the emperor's new clothes. *Journal of Educational Thought, 44*(3), 229–257. Retrieved from http://www.proquest.com/libraries/academic/databases/sociology.html

Boyle, M. (2013, August 5). President Obama's disastrous counterterrorism legacy. *Guardian.* Retrieved from http://www.theguardian.com/commentisfree/2013/aug/05/obama-legacy-shadow-wars

Bracey, G. (2009). The Bracey Report on the Condition of Public Education, 2009, *Education Policy Research Unit, 1(1),* 1–24.

Brown, O., Jr. (2013). The legal murder of Trayvon Martin and New York City Stop-and-Frisk Law: America's war against black males rages on. *Western Journal of Black Studies, 37*(4), 258–271. Retrieved from http://www.proquest.com/libraries/academic/databases/sociology.html

Carr, P. R., & Porfilio, B. (2009). The 2008 presidential campaign, democracy, and media literacy. *International Journal of Critical Pedagogy, 2*(1), 119–138.

Carr, P. R., & Porfilio, B. (Eds.). (2011). *The phenomenon of Obama and the agenda for education: Can hope audaciously trump neoliberalism?* Charlotte, NC: Information Age.

Carr, P. R., & Porfilio, B. (Eds.). (2015). *The phenomenon of Obama and the agenda for education: Can hope (still) audaciously trump neoliberalism?* (2nd ed.). Charlotte, NC: Information Age.

Chomsky, N. (2013, August 17). The U.S behaves nothing like a democracy. *Salon.* Retrieved from http://www.salon.com/2013/08/17/chomsky_the_u_s_behaves_nothing_like_a_democracy/

Foster, B. J. (2013). The fossil fuels war. *Monthly Review, 65*(4), 1–14.

Giroux, H. A. (2009, April 29). Youth and the myth of a post racial society under Barack Obama. *Truthout.* Retrieved from http://truth-out.org/archive/component/k2/item/83774:youth-and-the-myth-of-a-postracial-society-under-barack-obama

Giroux, H. A. (2013, September 4). Hope in a time of permanent war. *Truthout.* Retrieved from http://www.truth-out.org/opinion/item/18578-hope-in-a-time-of-permanent-war

Giroux, H. A. (2014, April 26). Neoliberalism's war on democracy. *Truthout.* Retrieved from http://www.truth-out.org/opinion/item/23306-neoliberalisms-war-on-democracy

Goodman, A., & Shaikh, S. (2013). Obama vows to seek Guantanamo closure, but immediate action could prevent hunger strikers' death. *Democracy*

Now. Retrieved from http://www.democracynow.org/2013/5/1/obama_vows_to_seek_guantnamo_closure

Hairston, T. W. (2013). Continuing Inequity through Neoliberalism: The Conveyance of White Dominance in the Educational Policy Speeches of President Barack Obama, *Interchange, 43*(3), 229–244.

Hudson, A. (2014, May 30). "Bush's fourth term continues": Guantanamo, torture, secret renditions; indefinite detention. *Truthout.* Retrieved from http://www.truth-out.org/news/item/24030-bushs-fourth-term-continues-guantanamo-torture-secret-renditions-indefinite-detention

Maruthappu, M., Ologunde, R., & Gunarajasingam, A. (2013). Is health care a right? Health reforms in the USA and their impact upon the concept of care. *Annals of Medicine and Surgery, 2*(1), 15–17.

McCoy, W. A. (2014). Surveillance and scandal: Weapons in an emerging array for U.S. global power. *Monthly Review Press, 66*(3), 70–81.

McCrisken, T. (2012). Justifying sacrifice: Barack Obama and the selling and ending of the war in Afghanistan. *International Affairs, 88*(5), 993–1007.

Miller, T. (2012). The individual mandate: Ineffective, overreaching, unsustainable, unconstitutional, and unnecessary. Retrieved from http://www.aei.org/wp-content/uploads/2012/03/-the-individual-mandate-ineffective-overreaching-unsustainable-unconstitutional-and-unnecessary_080931954931.pdf

Mora, R., & Christianakis, M. (2011). Charting a new course for public education through charter schools: Where is Obama taking us? In P. R. Carr & B. Porfilio (Eds.), *The phenomenon of Obama and the agenda for education: Can hope audaciously trump neoliberalism?* (pp. 97–120). Charlotte, NC: Information Age.

Onosko, J. (2011). *Race to the Top* leaves children and future citizens behind: The Devastating effects of centralization, standardization, and high stakes accountability, *Democracy & Education, 19*(2), 1–11.

Ravitch, D. (2010). The myth of charter schools, *The New York Review of Books*, (November 11). http://www.nybooks.com/articles/archives/2010/nov/11/myth-charter-schools/

Rohde, D. (2012). The Obama doctrine. *Foreign Policy, 192*, 65–69.

Scahill, J. (2013, October 29). Obama presidency marred by legacy of drone program. *Mother Jones.* Retrieved from http://www.motherjones.com/politics/2013/10/obama-drone-counterterrorism-war-legacy

Street, P. (2014). Obama's whitewashed World War 2. *The Official Website of Paul Street.* Retrieved from http://www.paulstreet.org/?p=1209

Wagle, T. & Theobald, P. (2011). Connecting communities and schools: Accountability in the post-NCLB era. In P.R. Carr & B. Porfilio (Eds.), *The phenomenon of Obama and the agenda for education: Can hope audaciously trump neoliberalism?* (pp. 249–263). Charlotte, NC: Information Age.

Young, S., & Schwartz, M. (2014). Healthy, wealthy, and wise: How corporate power shaped the Affordable Care Act. *New Labour Forum, 23*(2), 30–40.

INDEX